UP, DOWN & OUT!

AUTOBIOGRAPHY OF
Norman William Palmer

First published in Great Britain as a softback original in 2021

Copyright © Norman William Palmer

The moral right of this author has been asserted.

All rights reserved.

No part of this publication may be reproduced, stored in a retrieval system, or transmitted, in any form or by any means, without the prior permission in writing of the publisher, nor be otherwise circulated in any form of binding or cover other than that in which it is published and without a similar condition including this condition being imposed on the subsequent purchaser.

Typeset in Dante MT Std

Editing, design, typesetting and publishing by UK Book Publishing

www.ukbookpublishing.com

ISBN: 978-1-914195-69-3

DEDICATION

To my family and all the wonderful people I have had the privilege and pleasure of meeting over my life-time

UP, DOWN & OUT!

"EAT YOUR GREENS AND CARROTS!"

At the height of the Second World War conflict in 1943, in the month of May, I was born along with my twin sister, who would be christened Pamela Joy (and always called 'Pam' from then onwards). We were subsequently, constantly referred to as 'War Babies'. Our sibling sister, who was christened Barbara Margaret (and kept that name throughout her life), was born four years earlier. I was christened Norman William, a name I would be identified with and retained for the first sixteen years of my life. Our parents were my mum, Amy Doris (always referred to as 'Dolly'), and my dad, William (always known as 'Bill'). Our family name was Palmer.

Pam and I were both delivered by a midwife from what was then our home; a very modest semi-detached three-bedroomed house my parents rented, with a small garden at the rear, located approximately three miles from the centre of the idyllic seaside coastal town of Herne Bay, with its reputation for having the world's first freestanding clock tower, pebble beaches and North Sea, in the County of Kent.

Very much regarded then, as later, as the 'Garden of England' on account of its moderate climate, lush vegetable and fruit farms, and famous hop-picking.

Our birth was a fairly straightforward procedure with no complications (although I would go on a couple of weeks later to undergo a twisted hernia operation with the performing surgeon circumcising me at the same time, a procedure quite uncommon in those days and yet another characteristic that would mark me out as different). I was the first to see the light at the end of the tunnel before my sister, and consequently pushed my way out, making a rapid exit and arriving in the world ten minutes before her! In so many ways, as our individual lives eventually developed, this would come to represent something of a metaphor in relation to our individual futures.

Pam would grow up to become a somewhat shy, introverted and at times, rather withdrawn person, although enjoying the advantage of having dark, attractive physical features (similar to Mum). On the other hand, I was almost from the point of conception, confident, outgoing and rather pushy; characteristics that would come to define me throughout my life. From a very early age, I was already growing out of wearing what were second-hand clothes, rapidly shooting up to nearly six foot by the time I had reached ten years old. I was therefore very much regarded as a skinny lad; giving the firm impression of someone slightly under-nourished, although my deep blue eyes and very blond hair (physical characteristics I had inherited from my dad), often prompting observations by others as being a rather moderately good-looking boy.

Our elder sister, Barbara, Mum and Dad's first child, was very beautiful; combining the very best physical characteristics of both our parents and was very much regarded as the 'Apple of my dad's eye'. In consequence, they would go on to enjoy a very close relationship throughout his life, and during her teens Barbara would also win a Herne Bay Beauty Pageant, clearly something that made my dad feel exceptionally proud.

Our house was very modestly and sparsely furnished. It had no central heating (just one small fireplace in the sitting room) or modern-day appliances like a washing machine, dish washer, fridge, microwave or telephone, and certainly not a television – a rare, quite modern, privileged item for most households in those days, although we did gather around one of our well-off neighbours' tiny black and white TV set, to witness the Queen's Coronation in June 1953. We did, however, have the luxury of a bathroom, and on extremely cold nights, if we were lucky, a hot water bottle to take to bed with us. Our main source of household entertainment at the time was the wireless (radio) and we would often spend many happy, contented and idling hours listening to programmes like 'Workers Playtime' and 'Two-way Family Favourites'.

Our house was situated in an avenue adjacent to large open fields with trees and a few ponds dotted here and there which, at certain times of the year, contained spawning tadpoles, newts and other small fish which we would enjoy exploring. It was here, together with neighbourhood friends, we would spend many happy and enjoyable evenings, weekends and school holidays, playing childhood games like: 'Cowboys and Indians', 'Doctors and Nurses' and a wide variety of other activities. We certainly had no toys or television

(Computers, iPad and iPhone had not even been invented). We consequently grew up being very independent and self-reliant and quite creative when it came to leisure-time pursuits.

Even at the tender age of six, I was already beginning to take the lead in organising Avenue sports and other activities; an early indication perhaps of what was to come. A rare treat, however, for Pam and I during those formative years, was the occasional Saturday morning trip to the town's Odeon Cinema to watch what we fondly called, 'the flicks', and very infrequently over the summer period, excursions to the beach to swim in the very cold waters of the North Sea, even at that time of the year. Other occasions we would also become very excited at the prospect of enjoying the very occasional roller-skating outing on Herne Bay's famous pier. But that was often an expense considered to be too excessive for our parents, given that the household financial budget was run on a very limited and tightly controlled basis and we were therefore, by definition, regarded as poor and low working class.

Dad, however, had a very compact allotment, together with one apple tree in our relatively small back garden where he dedicatedly grew and cultivated a wide range of organic vegetables and fruit – something that would go on to be a much sought-after necessity for many – for us, it was part of our accepted everyday food and we came to regard it as quite normal. The by-word in the household at the time was always: "Eat your greens and carrots because they will benefit you in later life". Home grown vegetables were invariably complemented by a daily diet of rabbit which Dad caught locally most days using traps. Other meats during those war years were out of the question and it had been a number of years since the beginning of the War that food rationing had been introduced and formed part of everyday life. Our somewhat poor circumstances meant that we were also the beneficiaries of weekly food coupons which could be exchanged for goods in local shops, the butchers, bakers, as there was no such thing as 'supermarkets'. Butter was also a very rare commodity then, so inevitably we grew up with 'Stork margarine' on our bread. One very rare exception was when our fairly financially comfortable uncle and aunt from London visited us one Christmas year, bringing with them a reasonably large sized chicken to serve as the main course for Christmas Day – it was the very first time in our lives that we had experienced such an extravagance and a meat dish that as a result I would always go on to consider it my favourite.

When rationing finally ended after the war years, we were for the very first time able to buy chocolate, and despite our limited finances, Pam and I would demolish very quickly what were called chocolate 'wagon wheels'. A combination, therefore, of both good organic vegetables and fruit and rabbit, meant we never went hungry despite our relative poverty; the only few occasions were when, for six months, Mum and Dad separated with her going to London, but we were still fortunate to have very caring neighbours either side of our back-yard garden fence who ensured that we did not go without food for long periods.

Mum was a fabulous cook, a genuine 'Delia Smith' of her time and she could, with much ease, conjure up most days yet another different 'rabbit' meal. Her speciality, however, was her amazing moreish deserts: gooseberry, strawberry, apple pies etc. (also grown in Dad's small back-yard allotment) which were simply something to die for! In spite of very limited financial resources, she was always able to bake some of the most spectacular cakes. As kids we would often gather around the kitchen table to take turns, each licking the cake mixture leftovers around the bowl. Whenever we would enquire that day about the 'afters' (dessert), Mum's response was always the same: "Wait and see!"

Dad was always highly committed and devoted to his gardening, and during war years when horse-drawn carts were still being used to make local milk and coal deliveries, he would, shovel in hand, inevitably be the first to beat the neighbours into gathering up any horse manure that may have been deposited on the Avenue Road outside the house for his beloved rhubarb (again, often served as a main ingredient for yet another of Mum's delicious pies!).

Our poverty also extended to us wearing for much of our early years, second-hand clothes, usually handed out to us by the local Herne Bay Branch members of the Women's Royal Voluntary Service. I remember vividly arriving on my first day at Secondary School, wearing the compulsory maroon school uniform with the name 'John Oliver' stitched into the collar of the jacket. It was not surprising that as we matured, Pam and I would maintain a life-time penchant for new, smart, fashionable clothing.

Dad was a quite tall man, physically strong, somewhat muscular and definitely very proud of his masculinity. He possessed a very outgoing personality and had a 'wicked' sense of humour (when he was in the right mood in those days). Dad was, in every sense, 'a man's man'. He was, like many of his generation, a very strict disciplinarian; rules, as far as he were concerned, were rules to be obeyed without question and as such he was extremely forthright in both his views and attitude (something I would go on to inherit myself). Despite his somewhat intimidating verbal behaviour, Dad never once laid a hand upon us physically to punish us for any mischief we happened to be involved in at the time; yet corporal punishment in many homes and schools especially, formed part of everyday life. Nevertheless, there were many times when, owing to my boisterous behaviour, I suspected he was sorely tempted. This was also a time when the death penalty for murder was still in force.

Dad's life, however, was sadly blighted by his on-going epilepsy and consequently frequent severe fits (a health problem easily treated later in life but considered very serious in those days). One of his earlier epileptic fits had led to him being discharged early from the Army when, unconscious at the time, he fell on his rifle butt, knocking out most of his teeth in the process, ultimately leaving him wearing false dentures for the rest of his life.

This condition inevitably led to him suffering very dramatic mood swings and as kids growing up, we were never quite sure what kind of mood he would be in on any particular day. As a consequence of his epilepsy, I grew up accustomed to reacting very quickly whenever he had one of his many fits; grabbing any small wooden item I could lay my hands on to ensure that he did not swallow his tongue whilst he would be violently struggling, often in a semi-conscious state. This very unfortunate and debilitating condition led him to being unemployed for nearly 14 years, with just a small Government grant to support the family over this difficult period.

Nevertheless, he had two short periods of local employment; once as a porter at the local hospital and another job that gave him a lot of satisfaction, full-time Commissionaire at Herne Bay's Odeon Cinema, complete with magnificent uniform and epaulets – a place where he once managed to sneak the whole family in to watch, in full glorious Technicolour, the iconic movie: 'Gone with the Wind' – a four-and-a-half-hour epic with two intermissions, featuring film stars Vivien Leigh, alongside who was then regarded as the all-time favourite film star matinee idol, Clark Gable. As family members we would go on never to forget what a truly magical experience it was. And Clark Gable's role as Rhett Butler in the film ignited in me a passion and desire to become and pursue a career as a future film star myself, despite having a voice not dissimilar to Kenneth Williams of future Carry-On film fame.

Dad's condition was a constant source of irritation to him and on occasions led inevitably to severe depression. To combat this, he would engage daily in what he called his 'little flutter', betting on horse racing. In many ways this became quite a compulsive habit, principally to compensate for what I think he felt was his inadequacy in not supporting the family as principal breadwinner as other family men did at that time. Along with Mum, he had very little disposable income, so his minor gambling obsession resulted in him investing very small amounts of money into what he commonly referred to as the 'gee gees'. Nonetheless, he did work 'unofficially' (as this could have affected the very small Government 'hand-out' that they were in receipt of at the time should this have ever got out). This casual work was commonly referred to as working on the 'QT' (on the quiet) with him undertaking gardening jobs in the neighbourhood, cutting lawns and trimming hedges, something he became very proficient at whilst at the same time giving him a little bit of a 'back-hander' in terms of pocket money to supplement his meagre income. This would allow him the opportunity to bet on yet another horse that invariably failed to cross the finishing line!

It was not uncommon to see him crouched over the sitting-room table, fag in his mouth, his lifetime favourite being Weight's cigarettes (a habit that would eventually go on to have a devastating impact on his future health), pencil in hand, casting a discerning and critical eye over the racing pages of the Daily Mirror (our regular daily newspaper). His favourite jockeys being Lester Piggott (who would go on to be Champion Jockey many times), and Scobie Breasley.

Dad also had a very strict view about household pets, so when one day Pam and I asked him about the possibility of getting a dog, his reaction was immediate and highly predictable: "Dog, bloody dog, we can hardly afford to feed ourselves, let alone a bleeding dog!" Pam was still intent on asking him about the possibility of having a small hamster, but I managed in the end to persuade her to think otherwise.

Mum, on the other hand, was a relatively short person physically, had dark, attractive features, (that my twin sister Pam would go on to inherit), brown eyes and hair. In terms of personality, she was the direct opposite of my dad. They, nevertheless, perfectly complemented each other. Mum was in every sense of the word, a very gentle soul; quiet but an extremely kind person, although there were times when she could be somewhat over-sensitive. Despite any financial difficulties she may have been experiencing at the time, she was the kind of person who would literally give her last penny to someone she considered more disadvantaged than herself. I always felt these very noble and magnanimous qualities were very much influenced by Mum's own Salvation Army upbringing. In common with Dad, Mum also lost her teeth at an early age – it seemed it was quite common then for dentists to extract all your teeth, no matter how minor your problems. Consequently, Mum also wore dentures. She did occasionally smoke but, unlike Dad she was not a habitual smoker. For her it was 'special occasions' or 'high days and holidays'.

In spite of suffering frequent bouts of ill health herself, this never prevented her from working very hard all her life, especially during those early days in Herne Bay. Mum would go out doing part-time 'skivvying' cleaning jobs; scrubbing floors and steps to make ends meet and supplement the paltry income of the household and epitomised by a period of 'make do and mend'. It was inevitably very hard and at times, 'raw' work, but Mum was never a 'complainer' or 'moaner' (another characteristic that Pam would go on to inherit), she just took life in her stride and made the very best of things. A saying at the time was "A women's work is never done", and Mum was the absolute personification of that attitude throughout her relatively short, but extremely hard-working life.

Mum luckily recognised in me very early on, the more creative side of my character and encouraged this whenever she could. However, she also recognised certain flaws and warned me numerous times to guard against being too 'impulsive'. An emotion that would go on to dictate my feelings many times during my life, often with disastrous consequences.

When Dad's condition deteriorated at one point, Mum was pressured somewhat reluctantly at the time by people regarded as 'specialists' to have Dad 'sectioned' and taken for observation to a local mental institution, located in Canterbury some six miles away from the town. It was here, subsequently, where he spent the next six weeks undergoing treatment, including horrific 'electric' shocks, which I suspected haunted him for the rest of his life.

It was during this time, whilst I was attending Secondary School, that somehow news of my dad's illness and confinement in a mental institution got out. This resulted in a small, but very spiteful minority of peers, bullying me unmercifully most days, declaring loudly that my dad was in a 'Loony Bin' (loony being defined as someone 'mad' or 'silly') and calling me various names, including "Ad-Norm", an unpleasant abbreviation of Norman. From then onwards, I always felt that bullying should always be taken very seriously, knowing from intimate personal experience just how potentially harmful it could become to a person's future emotional development. And I remained ever vigilant to that kind of behaviour.

It was also over that period, with Dad away, that Mum herself with what at the time was considered a serious heart complaint, angina, was also admitted to the local hospital for a few days for medical treatment. It was another of those occasions when we were grateful for having such kind and supportive neighbours who cared for us during both our parents' absence.

In spite of what was a crippling condition of epilepsy, Dad was, quite remarkably, a very keen sportsman and loved his Saturday afternoon games of football that he played most weekends. Playing in the centre-half position, he was pretty good, especially heading a ball, given all his problems. Football, and generally most sports, held very little interest for me personally at the time and I knew this was a constant source of disappointment to him. These shortcomings on my part did not prevent Dad insisting that I accompany him regularly most Saturdays, to stand on the touchline in all weathers, with a bucket of very cold water and a sponge (to administer to any player caught up in a collision on the field) and also to hand out a dozen cut orange pieces to his fellow players at half-time.

Dad's disciplined approach extended to other household rules. You were always expected to be on time for meals and lo and behold if you were ever late at the table as you knew that resulted in you going to bed early, very hungry, having been prevented from eating your evening meal. We could also never commence eating until Dad gave us the nod and then always to use a knife and fork properly and never talk or open our mouths whilst eating. Furthermore, if for whatever reason you were unable to finish the main course, then you were denied any 'afters' (one of Mum's amazing desserts). "If you can't finish your vegetables, then you ain't going to get pudding," Dad would always declare, uncompromisingly. And you certainly never left the dining-room table until Dad had, once again, given his by now familiar nod.

Whenever we went out to play, invariably the close-by fields that always gave us so many pleasant hours of enjoyment, Dad always set the time you were to be back home, and heaven forbid if you were ever late, even by a minute or two. 'Rules were Rules' in my dad's household and both he and my mum set the bar very high when it came to those standards. Punctuality was therefore something very embedded in me at a very early stage.

This disciplined approach also extended to my mum's ageing mother, our grandmother, who lived in a house in Deptford, South London. Her husband, our grandfather, had died a few years earlier. She would rarely visit us in Herne Bay as she disliked my dad intensively and made this abundantly transparent, feeling always that her daughter, Doris, who had been given a good Salvation Army upbringing and also enjoyed a good education, and as such considered in those days 'middle-class', had quite definitely married below her status in life. The polar opposite of my dad, he coming from a very large, low working-class family background with over 20 siblings (some 'stillborn babies'), a common feature of pre-war England that ultimately led to us having many aunts and uncles on my dad's side of the family.

Our grandmother's very Victorian and disciplined approach to life meant that we always had to be on our very 'best behaviour' on the very rare occasions she would visit. Her attitude was very much reinforced by her strong opinion that "Little pigs should be seen and not heard". She often reminded me of one of the principal characters, Lady Bracknell, in Oscar Wilde's famous play, 'The Importance of Being Earnest'.

With, or without Grandmother, on the rare occasions we were out in what was regarded as the 'public domain', we were always expected to behave or otherwise risk getting one of Mum's famous 'looks to kill' expressions, which invariably meant that you were 'grounded' for the next day and confined to the house, with no opportunity to play outside.

Luxuries were inevitably very rare, but just occasionally Mum and Dad would take us to the local Herne Bay Branch of the British Legion where Dad was a member. Whilst he was engaged in a game of snooker and Mum gossiping with the other club members' wives, we were given what was then considered a scrumptious bag of 'Walkers' crisps, with a little 'blue' salt bag inside together with a bottle of our favourite soft drink, 'Vimto', a combination of flavours: grapes, raspberries and blackcurrants.

Dad, for all his faults, and there were many (notwithstanding his frequent mood swings), was a thoroughly decent, good man. He possessed a great deal of personal integrity and frequently revealed his very good sense of humour (which I hoped I would inherit from him, to say nothing of his very outspoken opinions). There were doubtless many times when he would be somewhat 'economic' with the truth and just occasionally he could be a tad dishonest. He was, however, very much regarded as a 'lovable rogue' wherever he went and in spite of his somewhat knavish behaviour, was extremely popular with people. Despite all his very evident outward disciplined approach to life, he was staunchly very protective of his family, at all times. This was made very abundantly clear in relation to our elder sister, Barbara, who Pam and I always considered to be his favourite member of the family.

Barbara had grown into a very attractive young woman by her late teens and had met and fallen in love with someone both my parents loathed and considered to be nothing more than an aggressive, fifties, Teddy Boy 'spiv' (a euphemism for someone regarded as 'flash'). Dad considered him uncouth, even by his own low working-class standards. He wore leathers and rode a motorbike which would infuriate my dad, especially when this man, Charlie, would leave the house quite late at night and ride off very loudly on his motorbike like a 'bat out of hell!' Barbara was evidently very smitten with him and despite Mum and Dad's obvious disapproval, decided to go ahead and get married to him. She was still very young at this stage, as was also Charlie, but she had subsequently discovered that she was already pregnant by him. In spite of the very strong joint feelings that my parents had, they nobly offered (given their own dire circumstances at that time), to help Barbara bring up the then unborn child with their support, so that she would not feel compelled to go ahead and marry Charlie. Nevertheless, she went ahead with a Register-Office style marriage that my parents attended, but very reluctantly.

Following the marriage, Barbara moved to South London almost immediately with Charlie and a few months later, Beverley was born (who became my first niece and subsequently went on in later life to establish herself as one of the most successful female 'traders' in the finance world). As my parents, especially my dad, had predicted, Charlie turned out to be a very violent thug and 'womaniser', who regularly physically assaulted Barbara, leaving her often bruised and battered. It was only a few months later, after we had ourselves moved and settled in South London, that this was discovered. At that time, Dad quickly moved Barbara, together with Beverley, to the house we were renting in New Cross Gate. This action did not prevent Charlie coming to the house late the following evening to retrieve Barbara and Beverley. In the melee that followed, Dad (who by that time was in his late forties and not in particularly good health), was physically very badly beaten up by Charlie, before the police had arrived, arrested Charlie and taken him away.

Barbara went on to get divorced and Charlie was recruited as a mercenary in Africa, which we all felt spoke volumes about the kind of brutal man he was. Barbara subsequently met a delightful man, Ron, and they married and had two children of their own, Mark and Sharon. They in turn got married and had children of their own. However, throughout her upbringing, Ron always treated Beverley as very much his own child. Well into their eighties, Ron and Barbara remained very happily married.

This episode in Dad's life demonstrated, very dramatically, despite the very obvious physical risks to himself, that as far as he was concerned, 'family was family' and as head of the household, he would go to any length to protect them.

At one unforgettable and traumatic period, when Pam and I were around ten years old, Mum and Dad separated for over six months, with Mum going to London to stay with her own mother in Deptford. We never then, or subsequently, knew why she took the action she did. It is possible that she could have simply reached boiling point over Dad's unpredictable behaviour, but it was a subject that was never discussed and remained forever a mystery. For all of us, however, it was a very unsettling and devastating time, and whatever the circumstances that had led to this situation, the pain on Dad's face over those difficult months without Mum was very self-evident.

By now he was a very lonely figure and would spend many days writing yet another pleading letter to my mum, begging her to return. At the time Dad coped with us as well as he could, given the circumstances, but Mum had become the familiar 'anchor' in his and our lives and therefore we were very confused and bewildered. For us it was an extremely painful sight to witness quite regularly, a normally strong, masculine man, reduced to uncontrollable emotions and frequently in floods of tears. Such distressing scenes inevitably influenced the lives of us all as we grew up.

Mum eventually returned to the home and life, once again, took on a semblance of normality with Dad still pursuing his daily 'flutter' on the horses (despite promises to the contrary that if Mum returned, he would give up the habit), but now actively seeking full-time employment, having been buoyed by Mum's return to the matrimonial home.

Despite all those emotional problems, I still had very fond memories of what I considered to be happy and carefree days, especially during my Junior School years. I was totally infatuated with our class teacher, a Miss Hampshire, when peers teased me unmercifully about being the teacher's 'pet' as I regularly escorted her part of the way home, as she lived near our house, carrying her school briefcase. And I remember particularly her telling words: "Now, Norman, if you want to grow up to be a gentleman, you should always open doors and stand on the outside of the pavement for ladies. That is considered to be very polite." Her wise words would never be forgotten throughout the rest of my life. Along with other Junior School class members, I would always hang on to her every word as she shared with us, in the classroom, the moving story by Johanna Spyri about 'Heidi and Peter' from an Alpine village in Switzerland.

Reminiscent of Junior School were sports events frequently held more often than not on inclement days, when we would sit collectively in class and resight the rhyme, "Rain, rain, go way. Come back on another day". Predictably, it would continue to pour 'cats and dogs' for the rest of the day!

One aspect that we all intensely disliked during those formative years were school dinners (lunch), something our parents didn't have to pay for. Despite the occasional main course that would represent a pleasant departure from our daily diet of rabbit, we all loathed a dessert that we nicknamed 'frogspawn' (a kind of semolina). Even the addition of a dollop of strawberry jam still left it tasting revolting, but the school dinner matron was always regularly on guard, with wooden ruler in hand, to ensure we all gulped it down without complaint!

It was around the age of 10 that I also encountered some quite serious health issues. I had two three-week spells, in the local hospital, being treated for acute double pneumonia. The second visit was very much a 'touch and go' situation, medically, and created considerable anxiety for my mum and dad and my sisters. Although I eventually made a full recovery, I was nevertheless still left with a permanently damaged left lung, that in turn led ultimately to me experiencing severe respiratory problems in later years. This was followed a year later by a further trip to hospital to have my appendix removed!

It was also a time when we were not far away from what was the up-coming National Eleven-Plus Exams. These were, in so many ways, very crucial, and to some extent a life-changing educational moment that determined your future direction. Although I would go on to be what was termed a 'late developer', I was still making good progress at Junior School and regarded as being potentially bright, academically.

Dad's view and attitude to the up-coming exams were extremely explicit and as always forthrightly expressed: "Don't bloody well think, no matter how bleeding well you do, you will finish up going to some fancy Grammar School (which was located some six miles away in Canterbury), with a lot of 'swanky' and bloody 'posh toffee-nosed' kids, with ruddy hockey sticks, violins and piano lessons. You won't be going! So, you can put any bloody ideas you might have completely out of your head, okay?" The message was very clear. Didn't matter how well Pam and I might potentially do in the exams, our future lay in the local Secondary School and that, subsequently, was our fate and future destination!

Herne Bay Secondary School was located at a place called 'Greenhill' and the Psalm 'There is a Greenhill Far Away' was a constant reminder of just how far away it was! It was a return walking journey of some five miles that Pam and I undertook everyday Monday to Friday, in all weathers, including when there were very extensive snow drifts. No matter what, we had to walk that intrepid journey every day, taking over one hour each way. It was a further two years before eventually the introduction of school bus transport which, fortuitously for us at the time, we were able to take for free on account of our perceived impoverished situation at home.

I thoroughly enjoyed Herne Bay Secondary School, and even though I was rather envious of the kids who took the bus from town every day, dressed in their extremely impressive Grammar School Uniforms heading for Canterbury, I had no regrets whatsoever about where I was. We were, however, blessed with some exceptionally good teachers and I quickly formed what would become quite close relationships with several members of my peer group.

It was not long before I was taking an active role in anything creative and performing arts was especially something that attracted me enormously. My personal aspirations still fixated on becoming the next Clark Gable! Before our future unknown geographical re-location, I threw myself fully into two school stage versions, as a member of the chorus, of Gilbert and Sullivan's Operas, 'The Pirates of Penzance' (with the memorable chorus: 'With Cat-Like Tread'), together with 'H.M.S. Pinafore' (and the chorus line, 'Sweet Little Buttercup, Dear Little Buttercup, I'.)

Out of school I was also a very enthusiastic choir member for quite a few years at the local church, Saint Bartholomew's, although I subsequently became completely disillusioned with religion in general (despite going on to hold strong spiritual feelings). Within two years of joining the choir, I had been elevated to Head Chorister, having a fairly good soprano voice (although never in quite the same league as the future Welsh soprano, Aled Jones). I was once nevertheless given the rare honour of being invited to sing solo at Canterbury Cathedral in the presence of the then, Archbishop of Canterbury, Dr Geoffrey Fisher.

For relatively brief period I was a regular attender at the local Sea Cadets Corps, I think primarily just to please my dad, who I always felt considered my artistic pursuits somewhat 'namby-pamby'. As it transpired, it was a rather short-lived association, as I persistently hoisted the Union Jack up the wrong way and after my third miserable attempt was ceremoniously kicked out!

One day, just prior to our fourteenth birthday, Pam and I were in for a complete and somewhat devastating shock! Dad had applied and been successful in securing a full-time position in a hospital in South London, as a porter. Naturally, we were both pleased for him. He had suffered very badly over many years and here was a golden opportunity for him to make a fresh start.

Nonetheless, we were, on hearing the news, quite traumatised as we were just beginning to put down what we considered to be semi-permanent roots and relationships with many local friends and both enjoying a school that we found rewarding and supportive. Yet here we were on the brink of being wrenched away from what had become our truly beloved seaside town, Herne Bay; its myriad, very happy and contented memories, including the occasional double whopper ice-cream and pink candy floss!

The Capital City of London, where we were ultimately heading, could have been the other side of the moon for all we cared at that moment in time. We had had only one brief experience of London a few years earlier when Pam and I took part in an organised school trip to visit the Festival of Britain; a National Exhibition that was located on the South Bank of London, with the aim of promoting a feeling of recovery, following many austerity years during World War Two. We were so impressed by all the new, innovative items that were exhibited, as well as the journey to and from London by steam train, which completed what for all of us taking part, was a perfect and very exhilarating day.

After all the trials and tribulations, this move represented something of a unique fresh start for Mum and Dad and this was very much reflected in their feelings and outlook. For that reason alone, we were both extremely happy for them, despite our own personal misgivings about the impending move.

For Pam and me, however, inwardly, this news was like a second world war 'bombshell' dropping on us and the prospect of this sudden, almost immediate and rather unexpected move, left us feeling genuinely intimidated, combined with an enormous sense of trepidation and anxiety for what was an uncertain future that lay ahead!

LONDON – DIRTY, SMOG-RIDDEN AND "ALL SHOOK UP"!

When we arrived in London a few weeks later, it was a city very much as we had anticipated: dirty, smog-ridden (this being a short period before Parliament's 'Clean Air Act' Bill was fully implemented). It was also heavily populated compared to anything we had previously become accustomed to. For Pam and me, this represented the opposite from wide-open spaces and relatively small semi-rural community we had come to associate as normal back in our cherished Herne Bay. In spite of my own initial fearful reaction, I would eventually go on to adopt London as a city that I would in time come to regard as home, enjoying its exciting, vibrant, multi-cultural environment.

Our house in South London was located in an area called New Cross Gate. A modest three-bedroomed terraced Edwardian-style house that Mum and Dad had rented in advance before our move. It was situated very close to an area called 'Cold Blow Lane', just a few yards away from the notorious Millwall Football Ground, appropriately named 'The Lion's Den'. A second division Football League Team at the time and characterised by its fearsome reputation!

Mum and Dad quickly settled down into our new surroundings, although Pam and I were still incredibly nervous and apprehensive. The house, although reasonably spacious, had a number of definite drawbacks compared to what we had become accustomed to in Herne Bay. There was no bathroom, just a metal bath that hung on the back-garden wall, so that inevitably resulted in us having what we came to regard as weekly 'wash down' nights.

Yet more concerning for us was the fact that we had to use an outside toilet, located just adjacent to the small backyard. Consequently, we had visions of having to go out in the dark, in all weathers, whenever we happened to be 'caught short'. Dad, of course, brushed aside all these anxieties on our part with his, by now, typical attitude: "Put some bloody backbone into you!" adding, "Especially as there ain't going to be any more compulsory Military Service in the future which I think is a ruddy mistake". I was personally mightily relieved that I wouldn't face the prospect when I got to 18 years of age of going on to what I considered to be two wasted years, 'square bashing', although at the time kept those thoughts firmly to myself.

Although Dad had his full-time hospital porter job, Mum had also, by this time, secured a part-time job with a cleaners' shop locally, thus the household disposal income over this period was better than anything we had enjoyed earlier. This did not stop Dad insisting that he wasn't going to waste stupid money on, as he put it, "Bloody silly soft toilet paper!" Instead, he would always cut-up his regular daily newspaper, 'The Daily Mirror', into square pieces and hang them on a hook on the inside of what we came to regard as the 'outside privy'. From that moment onwards, I was always concerned that I would grow up with the 'Daily Mirror' indelibly printed on my bottom!

The back yard was exceptionally small, even in comparison with our garden in Herne Bay, and there was certainly no space for any kind of fruit or vegetables to be grown. Meanwhile, Dad was settling into his new job, which seemed to give him a lot of personal satisfaction after so many years in the unemployment wilderness. It was also evident that he cut a popular figure with the people with whom he worked.

I loathed London initially and resented the move, feeling isolated and lonely most days. Mum had arranged for me to go to an all-boys School and Pam to an all-girls School, both located in the area. My school was perched at the top of a very steep hill, a journey of over a mile that I had to climb regularly every day. I quickly discovered, however, from my fellow school pupils, all of whom had been born and bred in London and consequently very 'street-wise', that my penis was not just for 'peeing!' This shocking revelation only served to underscore my complete naivety and total innocence at the time, especially in regard to my sexual knowledge. Later, when taking group showers with other boys, having always showered separately in my previous school, I felt something was desperately wrong with me. Not only did I have a circumcised penis, which the majority did not have, but also, I did not possess one single pubic hair at that point, whilst other boys looked like they had a veritable 'forest' between their legs! It seemed that not only was I to become a late developer, academically, but also physically!

In time, I became quite accustomed to the rough and somewhat verbally strong attitudes of several of my peers, in many ways a rite of passage for me, yet in spite of this still pursued with much enthusiasm my interest in the school drama section. This resulted in me being cast in what was intended to be a very emotional play, the title of which I could never remember. I was to play the principal role, portraying an elderly, somewhat delusional woman, complete with grey wig – my first real acting debut.

The Head of Drama was most impressed by all the cast members during rehearsal performances and particularly the emotional interpretation I had apparently given to the role. He subsequently entered us into a forthcoming Annual Dramatic Arts Area Festival, confident of our ability to compete well against other school drama groups in South London. The Festival itself being staged in a very large theatre in nearby Deptford and what was expected to attract a lot of bums on seats.

During the afternoon rehearsal I had already expressed concern to the Theatre Stage Manager about what I felt was a very wobbly set, given that the climax to the play necessitated me throwing open a door somewhat vigorously whilst delivering my final line. He completely dismissed these genuine concerns on my part and the performance duly went ahead in the evening as planned.

It was, as had been expected, a very full audience, including my mum, Pam and several aunties who had willingly come along to give their support. As always, Dad stayed away as he had no time for what he described as 'arty-farty stuff'. The play was going exceptionally well and building to its full climax with the audience following attentively every action and line delivered. My final act was to rush over to a door located at the rear of the stage set and fling it wide open, ushering in the final emotional words "I'm a mother no longer!". At precisely that point the entire set collapsed around me, taking off my grey wig in the process! It was not just the set that had collapsed, but also all members of the audience, including my family members who were splitting their sides with hysterical, uncontrollable laughter! This was meant to serve as my first tender steps into the world of dramatic arts and as events had unfolded, seriously undermined my burning and hopeful ambition of becoming the next Michael Caine. However, I could at least claim the surname of one of his famous roles; and not a lot of people knew that!

After the disastrous conclusion to the play, Mr Abercrombie, the Head of the School's Drama Department (whom we had nicknamed 'Mr Apple Crumble'), was absolutely furious, not so much with me or other cast members, but the Stage Manager who had earlier given us his full assurances about the set. Needless to say, we never went on to win the Festival Competition that night!

Identical to his strongly held views about our earlier educational paths, Dad was abundantly clear about our future direction after school. At aged 15, Pam and I could have chosen to stay on for an extra year to undertake what was then called GCSEs (General Certificate in School Education), but Dad clearly had other ideas.

I enquired one day, before reaching 15 (given my passion for drama and performing arts, generally), about the possibility of me applying for RADA (Royal Academy for Dramatic Arts). I would never forget Dad's response which came in the form of an outburst: "RADA, bloody RADA!" he bellowed, "that's a place for 'poofs' and 'girls' blouses'. You can put that bleeding idea completely out your head, my boy. You will leave school at 15, get a proper job and for once start contributing to the household budget, got it!" Any slight, lingering ambitions I might have had at that stage of my life were consequently 'flushed' down the outside loo, along with my dad's very clear feelings on the matter!

Dad would always attend Millwall Football Club's ground most Saturdays when they were playing at home (and when he was not required to undertake overtime at the hospital where he was still working as full-time porter), and inevitably became a 'die-hard' supporter. The Club had a justifiable reputation for aggression and the ground's name, 'The Lion's Den', together with the area, Cold Blow Lane, spoke volumes! Visiting players and supporters often felt highly intimidated and the experience for many would inevitably be like literally entering a 'Lion's Den'. It was therefore a common sight to witness fights breaking out between competing supporters on the nearby street where we were living.

Dad always wanted me to accompany him to the games, but always insisted that he position himself right behind the middle of the opposing side's goal mouth, whereas I always chose to spectate from the side of the club's ground. This chosen spot of his enabled him to constantly barrack and shout obscenities to the then long-suffering referees (paid a pittance in those days), and certainly nowhere near enough to have to contend with my dad's constant verbal abuse throughout the match on a regular basis. This frequent and very embarrassing behaviour was the primary motivation for me standing at the side of the grounds; there being no stadium seats in those early days.

In addition to his skills as gardener, Dad was also a very enthusiastic and quite experienced do-it-yourself handyman and this skill came in very useful when his porter job called for him to undertake some regular maintenance duties. Dad was also very adept and quite meticulous at wallpaper hanging and started covering most room walls in the house with a variety of wallpaper designs selected by Mum. Dad always enlisted my help (although he generally considered me quite incompetent), invariably getting me to stir the wallpaper mix and steady the ladder whilst he would balance himself, hanging a particularly long piece of wallpaper. I was, and continued to be, the exact opposite to my dad in so many ways and DIY was no exception – and I was totally hopeless at any half-hearted attempts I would make in the future. When, much later in life, I had married and felt compelled to make some feeble attempt at any outstanding odd job around the house, my then wife would insist: "You will only finish up getting super-glue all over everything, so get a proper professional in to do the work".

It was also following school, that I enrolled at a local Institute College for an evening course to improve my English and a three-month Pitman's shorthand and typing course, becoming quite proficient in the process, especially the typing. By the end of the course, I knew the keyboard off by heart. These skills learned at that time, would inevitably go on to hold me in good stead, particularly as in the future with the eventual introduction of computers, the keyboard being identical to that of a typewriter.

As predicted, along with twin sister, Pam, I left school at 15 with no certificates in hand, unlike many of my contemporaries at that time. However, I promptly got my first job as an Office Boy in a very large Publishing Company, Amalgamated Press, located just off the famous Fleet Street. My weekly salary was then five shillings a week of which three shillings had to be given to the household in line with Dad's ruling. Nonetheless, that still left a fairly reasonable and healthy balance, a time when my appearance and clothes were becoming increasingly important to me and a source of personal pride. My vanity often led me to feeling that I was very much 'the man about town' and I saw myself as being rather 'dapper' and 'de rigueur'. I also sought out what was in those days termed as 'barber's' shops, distinguished by their external colourful swirling pole. I favoured the 'Beatles' hair style look, being a self-confessed 'Mod' rather than 'Rocker'. At the completion of every barber's cut, however, was by now a familiar expression handed to customers. "Anything for the weekend, Sir?", a reference to 'under the counter' condoms that were difficult to come by, and particularly to someone of my young age.

It was also around the age of 19, a time when I felt subjected to some degree of peer pressure, that I began smoking.

Back then there was virtually no public education about the potential health hazards of smoking and it was also very much regarded as socially acceptable. Given my lung, and subsequent quite severe respiratory problems, it was a very unwise and unhealthy move. Over the next 25 years I would go on to be an exceptionally heavily addicted smoker, finishing up regularly smoking three packs a day. It was only as a direct result of my future wife's timely intervention that I gave up, after she astutely observed one day when I was wheezing going up the house stairs: "Bill, if you don't give up that filthy habit you will never make old bones". For months afterwards I had to go through a period of 'cold turkey', there being no such thing as 'patches' or any other support at that time. Finally, I succeeded in kicking the habit, but it would be many years before I was able to completely rid myself of the nicotine that had by now accumulated in my body. Had it not been for such wise words, I know I would not have lived as long as I have.

Dad continued supporting his beloved Millwall Football Club and his regular abuse of referees becoming something of a ritual by then. Yet, as another testimony to his personality and character, I recall very vividly one Saturday, following the end of the game and during our short walk back home, more evidence of this. It was customary, given the large crowds that the games would attract, for the police to appoint temporary 'Special Constables' to help with supervising the crowds of people after the game on their return home. On this occasion, Dad was about one hundred yards ahead of me, but within hearing distance. Suddenly, a Special Constable began to start manhandling a young kid who was basically just being somewhat boisterous, but otherwise quite harmless. Quickly, I saw my dad intervene, shouting to the Copper, "Put a bloody uniform on some people and they become right little 'Hitlers'. Leave the kid alone and bleeding well go and pick on someone your own size!", resulting in the Special Constable making a very quick exit from the scene. My dad had no idea that I had witnessed this event or even heard what he had said. The memory of that incident, however, remained firmly with me for a long time afterwards and was yet another occasion when I was proud of his actions.

Millwall Football Ground would also double-up and be converted every Saturday evening into what was then a very popular local Greyhound track. Predictably, most Saturday nights, given his propensity to gamble, Dad would invariably be 'off to the dogs', being located so close to where we were living, especially after his customary failure to bet on a winning horse that day. Dad's favourite traps were two and four that he regularly bet on. If the hounds succeeded in crossing the winning post in first and second place in that order, or reverse order, you could potentially return home with a tidy sum in your back pocket. Inevitably, odds on, it would generally always be a case of hearing Dad curse loudly following a race: "Bugger! Someone has obviously fed those bleeding dogs before the start of the race!" Trap two and four dogs invariably destined to come trailing in last!

This period was also synonymous with what was known as 'The Swinging Sixties', the beginning of tumultuous change socially, culturally, scientifically, sexually. And also musically, characterised by popular artists like Elvis Presley and his 'All Shook Up!' and The Beatles 'A Hard Day's Night' songs. It was also in our household, two potentially life-changing introductions. Our first landline, a rather vulgar avocado-coloured telephone, and black and white television set. Every week, including Dad, we would be huddled around the small set to watch Bruce Forsyth compere the very famous and extremely popular 'Sunday Night at the London Palladium'.

This was also a time when I was beginning to take a very serious interest in classical music and remembered it as if it were yesterday, Dad's reaction when I took home my first EP (Extended Play) disc to be played on our 'Dansette' record player, a recording of Rodrigo's 'Guitar Concerto' (which would go on to be one of my favourite pieces of music). "Bleeding classical music, what next? What the bloody hell's wrong with the Beatles music" (which I also liked, anyway) "and who is this Rodrigo bloke, some ruddy Spanish Bull Fighter?" This did not, however, prevent me from going on to have a lifetime passion for classical music.

Meanwhile, our grandmother, on our mother's side of the family, who was a staunch Salvation Army supporter, holding the rank of Captain at her local 'Citadel', would always expect us from time to time, to accompany her to her local Deptford Branch and join in a rousing chorus of 'Hallelujahs', accompanied by several tambourines being shaken senselessly.

My grandmother and grandfather (he having tragically died a few years earlier from throat cancer and whom I remembered being a very quiet and gentle kind of person), were extremely comfortable, financially. Grandfather having worked his whole life in a fairly senior position within the National Gas Board Company. They had bought and owned outright their quite large, terraced house in Deptford (formerly a slum area), which was very well furnished, including what they regarded as their 'pride of place', a genuine and very highly valued 17th century, Queen Anne dressing table that apparently Grandfather had successfully bid for at auction several years earlier.

Before Pam and I had reached our twentieth birthday, our Grandmother had also passed away, following a short illness. When it came to the reading of her 'Last Will and Testament' held by her local solicitor, it was quite a revelation (and I suspected, shock, especially for my mum). Apart from a small sum of money to cover her funeral expenses, the house, its contents (including the Queen Anne dressing table) and personal items of jewellery etc., were all to be donated to the Salvation Army. My mum took this announcement typically in her stride with much stoicism, although Dad's expression on his face told us everything, without him uttering a word in front of us.

In spite of her devoted Christian commitment, I always felt this action totally at odds with her outward philosophy and principles. Yet, in many ways, it seemed a calculated and deliberate act of pure spitefulness on her part for my mum's audacity in marrying someone like my Dad, whom she always regarded as very much well below her own class. Dad's background being viewed as very low working-class, coming as he did from a very large extended family.

Had things turned out differently, financially, Mum and Dad could inevitably have been set up for the rest of their lives. But as events were to turn out, life continued much the same as it had done before. Yet, following Grandmother's passing, I never once heard ever again, either from my mum or dad, any criticism, rancour or bitterness openly expressed, let alone any further discussion about what appeared to be her deliberately contrived malicious actions.

Although Dad's mood swings were not as dramatic as they had been in the past, primarily due to better medication and the fact that he was holding down a full-time job he clearly enjoyed over what was now a very sustained period of time, there were occasions when inevitably he had his 'off days'.

By my late teens I had established quite a few local London 'mates', and occasionally would approach Mum and Dad with a view to inviting them back to the house for drinks. Mum was always keen on the idea being as she loved entertaining, as well as giving her the opportunity to display her many culinary skills. Dad, on the other hand, although in the end reluctantly agreeing, would always make a song and dance about it, questioning as to why I needed to bring mates back home in the first place.

However, when the night itself actually came along with mates already assembled in our front lounge (reserved for very 'special' one-off occasions), Dad would always turn out to be the real 'life and soul' of the party; cracking jokes (often very dirty ones!), full of laughter and merriment and generally behaving very *'bonhomie'* throughout the evening. My mates considered me extremely lucky for having such a humorous and ebullient dad. I would always nod approvingly, but at the same time would be thinking to myself, 'You don't have to live with him every day!'.

Because of Dad's extended family, we consequently had several cousins. One I was always particularly curious about was my cousin Gordon, him being about 12 years older than Pam and me. He was in the music business, having been taught the piano at an early age and being the son of a family of three, with two musically gifted sibling sisters, nieces Delia and Jillian. We always regarded their parents (our aunt and uncle) as quite rich and comfortable. They lived in a very pleasant semi-detached house in Merstham, in the picturesque County of Surrey that we only visited on a few occasions.

Gordon, or David (his middle name that he had adopted professionally), was singer Dorothy Squire's personal pianist and constantly accompanied her on many tours, nationally and overseas. Gordon had a 'gay' partner, although my aunt and uncle always spoke about him as his 'business partner', and it was a subject never discussed in the family. It had only been a few years earlier in 1957, that a Government-commissioned report, 'The Wolfenden Report', had concluded that: "Homosexual behaviour between consenting adults in private should no longer be considered a criminal offence".

Gordon spent much of his late twenties in Soho, London; an area that had become associated with music during that period called 'Tin Pan Alley'. He eventually left England and settled in Los Angeles in the USA to pursue his musical career. It was rumoured (although I subsequently never found any evidence to support this claim), that when experiencing difficult times, financially, he supported himself by participating in 'gay' porno movies on account of him allegedly being well-endowed. Gordon, however, would eventually return to the UK when in his late fifties.

Following my year's apprenticeship as office boy, I was retained by the Company as a Publicity Assistant – by that time, the Company having been taken over by the Daily Mirror Group and re-titled 'Fleetway Publications'. As a general assistant, I was called upon to undertake numerous duties and one event that loomed large was the launch of a new young women's magazine, 'Honey', in 1960. To celebrate this, a showbiz concert was staged at London's famous Albert Hall. During what was a momentous day, I brushed shoulders with an array of very famous musical celebrities, including Cliff Richard, Alma Cogan, Dusty Springfield, Bert Weedon, Anthony Newland, Marty Wilde and many others. Had I the sense to collect their autographs on that day, I would have made a small fortune years later.

It was also around the age of 19, that I was starting to make good headway professionally and had been appointed to a post in a small advertising agency, Mayfair Advertising, on London's embankment, commuting each day by bus from our home in New Cross Gate. It was my very good fortune to have as my boss, a lady called Irene Taylor. She was in her early fifties and was a spinster at the time and remained so for the rest of her life. She was both a joy and delight to work with and a very empowering type of person. Irene would be one of many female bosses I would come to work with over the years. This early relationship would ultimately help shape my own attitude towards equal opportunities and much of my own future thinking.

Irene's support and nurturing meant that I made a very rapid advance within the small advertising company and was finally given the status of Account Executive. This entailed me having a small portfolio of clients to support using the Company for their advertising purposes; two of the most important being Claude Rye Ball Bearings and Prout Sailing Boats. It was certainly at that point in my life I felt I had found my niche, professionally, and that my future career looked both promising and secure. I was also earning a very good monthly salary, yet still living at home in New Cross Gate, thus leaving me with a reasonable amount of disposable income.

After my promotion, Irene spoke to the Managing Director of the Company and they jointly agreed that once a week I should attend a Day Release College in West London to enhance my knowledge and understanding of printing and graphic arts, with the Company paying for the course. This initiative was typical of Irene's kindness and thoughtfulness. I accepted the offer, not appreciating that this decision would go on ultimately to totally change my future direction in life.

After a few weeks at the college, I became friendly with a fellow student, Bill, who like me, was the same age and also working for another advertising company but undertaking voluntary youth work in the evening. It was also at that point in my life I had also completely adopted the name 'Bill', never to be known again as Norman, although acquiring a variety of other 'nicknames' throughout my life.

Bill asked me if I would be interested in becoming involved with voluntary youth work and I accepted, although not really giving too much consideration or thought as to what exactly I was getting myself involved with. A few nights later, Bill accompanied me to a youth centre in Camberwell, South London, an area regarded as deprived at the time, dominated by high-rise Council block buildings and housing predominately working-class families.

I somehow took to the work quite easily although those early days represented something of a steep learning curve for me and I was very dependent upon advice and support. The full-time youth worker at the centre was a truly inspirational man, John Stanton, who was in his late twenties and a devoted Catholic, although he never wore his religion on his sleeve. He was an incredible role model for whom I had much admiration.

Being 'street wise', with the external appearance of 'toughness', were general characteristics that marked out most of the membership; verbal, as well as physical aggression were familiar trademarks that were never far from the surface.

John's exceedingly caring and patient persona and calming personality was not lost on the young people, and they responded extremely well to his style of leadership and he was obviously very much respected. His remarkable interpersonal skills would go on in the future to guide my own feelings and actions.

Whilst still maintaining progress in my full-time job, with Irene continually kind and supportive, I had by that time thrown myself totally into my evening and what would eventually become weekend activities with the youth centre. Again, I was extremely fortunate to be working under John's guidance and there were no doubts about his commitment to the young people. For the first time in my life, I was involved assisting in myriad activities I had never undertaken before: Camping, Pony-Trekking, Sailing, and regularly accompanying the centre's football team to matches.

Using my advertising experience, particularly in terms of layout, design and copywriting, I started a club magazine which became very popular, with several members contributing articles etc. Unbeknown to me, John entered the magazine in a National Youth Club Competition and a few weeks later, we were informed that out of several hundred entries, the magazine had been awarded top prize. I was subsequently invited to represent the club and to receive a trophy from the Duke of Gloucester at St James' Palace in London the following month. Not fully appreciating at that time, this would be the first of many encounters with 'Royalty'.

Doing voluntary work in a youth centre was forming a major part of my life and by now I had established very good relationships with many of the young people. Even Dad was impressed by what was now occupying most of my leisure-time: "Doing something at long last that will make a man out of you, rather than all that other bloody nonsense, drama and bleeding classical music". Mum, as always, would be there to intervene and defend me, telling Dad that he should for once in his life acknowledge that not only was I making a potentially successful professional career for myself, but also undertaking voluntary work in my spare time that she felt would help young people "grow up to be decent and law-abiding, respectable citizens". This, however, never really seemed to 'cut much ice' with my dad.

With all this activity going on, including passing my driving test (at my second attempt) and still living with Mum and Dad in New Cross Gate, Pam had in the meantime met and fallen in love with someone at the local shirt factory, Rael Brook, where she and he both worked. His name was Alf, a rather large man, physically, a born and bred Yorkshireman and proud of his roots. After a whirlwind and relatively short courtship, they got married and went on to have three children, Stephen, Deborah and Gary. Both Stephen and Deborah would themselves go on later in life to get married and have children of their own.

Pam and Alf's life would sadly go on to be overshadowed by tragedy. Pam was born with an extremely rare blood group, rhesus negative. Unlike me, who possessed the most common blood group A, which I shared with much of the population. Pam and Alf were strongly advised, medically, under the circumstances, not to go ahead with any thoughts they may have harboured at the time for a planned third child after the births of Deborah and Stephen, as the specialists felt this could potentially result in a child being born handicapped. There being no scanners or other modern-day technologies at that time, and consequently any physical defects would only be discovered once giving birth. Pam and Alf, however, chose to ignore this advice and went ahead and had their last child, Gary. He was, as the specialist had warned, born with severe Spina Bifida (a congenital condition in which the spinal cord protrudes through a gap in the backbone that can lead to paralysis).

After many surgical operations, initially to correct some of these defects, Gary would go on to spend much of his life in callipers and later in a wheelchair. For all his problems he remained very cheerful and generally contented. Pam and Alf had also been warned that eventually his major organs would inevitably break down and there was almost 100% certainty of him not living beyond the age of 30.

Nevertheless, Pam and Alf went on to devote much of their time and effort over the next 30 years of their marriage, caring and ensuring wherever possible that Gary had the very best of opportunities, given what was to become his relatively short lifespan. Their dedication, self-sacrifice and nobility were something I would always admire. To accommodate Gary's handicapped needs later in his development, they were able to get their local authority to provide a specially adapted bungalow close to Gatwick Airport, where Pam, Alf and Gary would go on to spend the rest of their lives.

As forecast, Gary died in his very early thirties from a heart attack, but in his final year enjoyed a degree of independence when he was able to live in a residential home alongside other young people with difficulties similar to his own. He also had a girlfriend at that time, enjoying a very close relationship with her.

Gary's ultimate death, although predicted, was nevertheless traumatic for Pam and Alf, from which they never really fully recovered. It was also, a very sad time for the whole family. Gary was finally laid to rest in the grounds of Surrey & Sussex Crematorium, a place that would become very significant many years later.

My voluntary work now represented a period of intense activity and I had also enrolled to undertake a Voluntary Youth Leaders Training Course one evening a week. This would go on to be another life-changing experience! On one of the evening sessions, we were given details about the work of the National Voluntary Service Overseas (VSO) organisation (the UK's equivalent of the USA Peace Corps). I was totally captivated by the idea of young people (in most cases young people using their 'gap' year before going to university) to volunteer to work for one year on an assignment somewhere overseas, possibly Africa or the Far East. A future destination ultimately determined by the staff at HQ, dependent on the person's prior knowledge or experience.

I decided to write requesting an application, although seriously felt my background and limited academic skills would be a distinct disadvantage and impediment. But, I was reminded by Dad's home-spun philosophy on life: "If you don't bloody well ask, you don't get!" – that would also become something of a guiding principle throughout my life. To my utter surprise, I was in fact called for an interview one day a couple of months later in London. Despite my misgivings, I eventually received a letter informing me I had been selected and required to attend two further residential weekend courses along with other volunteers.

My selection was, in so many ways, a very significant 'watershed' moment in my life. I went on to discover that I was one of only a minority of young people who were not going on to university after their year overseas. This was a real morale boost to my self-confidence. When I shared my news with the family they were overjoyed; even Dad gave a

LONDON – DIRTY, SMOG-RIDDEN AND "ALL SHOOK UP"!

somewhat begrudging "Well done, son". At work, as with the youth centre where I was working voluntarily at the time, everyone was clearly delighted by my selection.

Irene shared my joy, but at the same time expressed her sadness at my impending departure. Typically, she saw the Managing Director a couple of days later and it was agreed to keep my post open whilst I was overseas for the one-year. Irene's actions epitomised the immense kindness and exceptional human qualities she possessed, and I considered myself extremely fortunate at that juncture in my life to be touch by the lives of people like her and John Stanton. Over the next few years, Irene and I remained constantly in touch until her untimely death twenty years later. Similarly, John and I would continue to be close personal friends for many years.

For me, however, I was confident that I was taking a very different direction in life, feeling there would be little prospect of me returning to the world of advertising. Also, I had already been approached with regards to undertaking a full-time unqualified post in a voluntary youth centre in Westminster, very close to the Houses of Parliament, after my return from VSO. This future opportunity would also give me the necessary practical experience I needed prior to what I hoped would ultimately lead to a full-time one-year training course at The National Youth and Community Training College that had been established by the Government.

A few weeks later a member of staff at VSO Headquarters wrote to me to say that I had been assigned to a Multi-Racial Mixed Gender School about six miles from the coastal town of Mombasa, in Kenya, East Africa. At that point I was not particularly troubled as to where I was destined, but just thrilled and overjoyed that I had been selected.

Shortly afterwards, I received a very informative letter from the Head Teacher of the School, St. Augustine's, Derek Bowtell, outlining what my duties and responsibilities entailed over the coming year, based upon the information he had received from VSO HQ. I was to act primarily as the House Master of the mixed Boarding School section located about three miles from the school, with the pupil age range from seven to eleven, basically Junior School age. Other duties involved me serving as his secretary (given my shorthand and typing skills), taking sports and also organising artistic events, including the annual Christmas nativity play, this being a predominately Christian faith-based School.

The sense of excitement at that time was palpable and I was already beginning to contemplate some of the activities I could undertake with the boarding youngsters who would become my principal responsibility. This opportunity also represented a first for me in that, other than a short trip to the Isle of Wight with the family, I had never travelled overseas before. Yet here I was just about to embark upon a 5000 miles flight to Nairobi, Kenya in East Africa.

Dad was still working at that point, but it was clear for all to see that his health had started to deteriorate. His epilepsy was firmly under control by this time, due to the introduction of new medication, and he no longer suffered from any more fits. It was his habitual smoking, however, that had finally caught up with him and he had been diagnosed by a local doctor with severe emphysema, exacerbated by chest problems which were now giving him times when he struggled for breath.

It was in August 1963, with all my inoculations – yellow fever, cholera – completed, bags packed, together with a small typewriter I had purchased, that all my family members accompanied me to Heathrow Airport before my long flight to Nairobi, Kenya, via Khartoum and Southern Rhodesia (as it was known in those days, now Zimbabwe) with BOAC (British Overseas Airways Corporation, before eventually becoming British Airways) to bid me *"Bon Voyage"*.

When the time came for me to finally say goodbye to the family and enter the Immigration area, I took one final glance back through the glass screen that separated us. Mum was, as always, looking very pleased, if not a little sad. Dad, on the other hand, who was by now looking very grey and much older, was waving and smiling very enthusiastically. His deteriorating health would be a constant source of concern to me over the coming year.

Two other VSO volunteers, Barry and Edwin, were my companions on the long flight, as they too had also been given one-year assignments in Kenya. Barry was to work at the YMCA in Nairobi as a general sports and activity worker, and Edwin was going to work in the Northern part of Kenya at a Divisional Government Office, undertaking general administration work. Over the somewhat brief two-day time we would all be together in Nairobi, before parting company to go to our respective assignments, we would give Edwin the nickname 'Tumu Tumu', which was to be his final destination in the country!

Collectively, we were very excited about our immediate futures, especially as our time in Kenya coinciding with the country's independence in December of that year (this was known locally as 'Uhuru', Swahili being the principal language predominately spoken, having been a former British Colony, and following years mired in violent terrorist activity perpetrated by what was commonly known as the 'Mau Mau').

Mum and Dad with baby Beverley

"HARAMBEE! – LET'S ALL PULL TOGETHER!"

Following our long flight, we were met at the airport and taken to a small Christian retreat in Nairobi where we were accommodated and given time to recover from our obvious jetlag. The temperature locally at that particular time being not that dissimilar to the UK summertime. Over the next two days, Barry, Edwin (by now accustomed to his adopted name) and I took the opportunity of visiting various renowned sites in the capital and even indulged ourselves one afternoon with high tea at Nairobi's famous five-star Stanley Hotel.

When it came for us to say our farewells, having by this time becoming quite close friends, we all agreed to meet up later during December in Nairobi to coincide with the Independence Celebrations that were planned to take place during that month.

Barry, consequently, stayed behind in Nairobi to take up his position in the local YMCA, with Edwin heading north by train for his Local Government posting. I was also boarding an early afternoon train to take me down to Mombasa; a

Port City at sea level (having the second largest population in Kenya), with a predominately wet, very dry, as well as humid climate, and characterised by its cosmopolitan population.

The long journey by train had to be undertaken overnight, so a single carriage compartment had already been booked for me, complete with bunk bed. The train journey ahead was almost comparable to the flight out, affording me a virtually new experience I had never previously enjoyed.

The single carriage I occupied had a very large window with spectacular panoramic views of the countryside and I was able to witness magical scenes of wildlife on the flat plains, whilst the steam train trundled its way slowly through the countryside to its ultimate destination. Game such as giraffe, deer and wildebeest became common sights and were for me truly something quite out of this world.

The restaurant carriage was located in the middle of the train and for both the evening meal and the following morning's breakfast, an attendant would walk up and down the corridor ringing a bell to announce that the restaurant was ready to serve its passenger guests.

When I eventually arrived at the carriage restaurant, it was yet another new and mind-boggling experience. Each restaurant table had been immaculately prepared with a starched white cotton tablecloth and napkins, complete with silver cutlery and cruet set, together with a crystal drinking glass. Set in the middle of the table was a small decoration of flowers and each dining section separated and draped either side with deep red velvet curtains.

The local Kenyan waiters, dressed top to toe in dazzling white uniforms, complete with white gloves and coloured fez hat, attended to our every whim. It was at that point I really did begin to feel I had stepped into a totally new world and certainly not the kind of experience I had expected as a volunteer! Before leaving Nairobi, I had, however, already been handed sufficient Kenyan Shillings (the local currency) to cover my meals en-route.

Around nine o'clock the following morning, rejuvenated after a good night's sleep and early, but most enjoyable full-English breakfast, we arrived at our final destination, Mombasa. Being at sea level it was extremely humid compared to the moderate temperature back in Nairobi. Derek Bowtell, the Head Teacher, was there to meet me. A relatively young, quite handsome man in his mid-thirties.

Derek initially took me off in his Land Rover to his apartment to meet his wife, Mary and to join them for lunch to generally discuss my duties over the coming year (their apartment being located a short distance from St. Augustine's School that we had passed en-route). The school itself was quite a substantially tall, two storey, blue and white coloured building and architecturally very pleasant on the eye, with lots of open corridors and a playing area situated at the front and rear.

After lunch he drove me about three miles, where he parked up his vehicle and led me down a marked pathway with long growing grass either side. After about 400 metres we passed a relatively small, wooden block that he pointed out to me as being where the school girl boarders were accommodated.

A further 100 metres down the track and we had reached what was quite a substantial wooden building, with cage-like windows and an area to the right of the building (where it seemed food was being prepared), leading to a veranda at the rear of the building that overlooked the close-by Indian Ocean. This was, as Derek explained, the Boys Boarding House where I would be spending much of my time for the next year.

It was here also that I was first introduced to the Matron, a quite elderly person who was a conspicuous former Christian Missionary in Kenya. My first impression of her was that she was a rather odd and quite strange individual who seemed to be very confused. Inside the building were about 30 young boys, between the ages of seven to 11, with whom I would be serving virtually *'in loco parentis'*, who greeted me enthusiastically with shouts of, "Hello, Sir. Welcome, Sir".

Within a few days of settling in, it became very apparent to me (and subsequently Derek, the Head), that my initial concerns about the Matron were not unfounded. It was very transparent that, sadly, she was suffering from severe dementia and would constantly wander around the building most nights exclaiming: "The Lord is here! Have no fear, the Lord is with us!". Her nightly behaviour was quite nerve racking, so it was hardly surprising that most of the residential boys felt very intimidated and frightened by this unnerving nightly activity. Derek took immediate action, and she was very promptly replaced by another Matron, a most delightful French-born lady, Estelle, with whom I would get along famously for the remainder of my stay and was most popular with the boarders.

At a quite early start each day, I would lead the boys down the marked pathway, joining the girls en-route (who had a Senior girl aged around 19, responsible for their supervision), to the main road where a bus would always be waiting to transport us to the school some three miles away. There were many occasions when I would return to the boarding house on my own, walking down this marked track, but ever watchful for the odd poisonous snake that could at any moment make an appearance! Snakes were my one phobia in life. The Kenyan chef at the boarding house did not help my confidence. He would tease me with graphic and often very exaggerated stories that would only ultimately confirm my constant fear of being bitten, particularly about the reputation of a very venomous snake he referred to as the 'Black Mamba'. "One bite of this and you literally have 30 seconds to live!" he exclaimed. It was not, therefore, very reassuring to know at that particular time, there was no antidote for this notorious snake's bite! Over the coming 12 months, however, I did witness many snakes, but like me they chose to keep their distance.

Along with the boarders I shared a meal that consisted of a local diet called 'Vgali', generally a maize mixture taken together with cooked vegetables, food that the boys invariably demolished like there were no tomorrows. I disliked it intensely and I was soon shedding quite a lot of weight. Once again, Derek quickly intervened and within a relatively short time I was eating more traditional English dishes.

Despite being fully occupied with my range of diverse duties, I always found sufficient time to relax on the boarding house veranda, enjoying a cup of tea. Here I would quite regularly type letters back home to the family and friends. I was especially concerned about Dad's health as Mum had already informed me that he had been advised by his local doctor to stop full-time work. It was not the kind of news I was hoping to hear.

This activity also extended to me writing quite regularly to VSO HQ and my contact there. This exercise was generally to let them know how things were progressing. If you, or any other volunteer, wrote something they felt could be shared in the regular monthly VSO Newsletter, it got published. Inevitably, none of my what I thought at the time were funny anecdotes ever got published. One very common sight whilst I would be beavering away quite happily on my little typewriter would be a familiar troop of local monkeys who would regularly traverse from one tree to the other in the nearby forest, howling furiously as they went on their way. It was clear that they did not consider me some kind of male equivalent to Jane Goodall!

Within a very short while, Derek, who was aware that I was in possession of a British Driving Licence, kindly presented me one day with a Vespa Scooter that he felt would help me get around a bit more, including also visiting the town of Mombasa, which up to that point I had not been able to do. Consequently, it would not be too long before I was tootling along on my Vespa, visiting the old part of Mombasa with its closely arranged buildings, influenced by Portuguese and Islamic architecture, and exploring the fascinating markets resembling unexplored 'Aladdin's Caves'. Also, to the famous Fort Jesus, a landmark iconic building as well as tourist attraction within the town.

I had also developed strong relationships with the boarders, as well as other pupils in the school and teaching staff, several of whom had become good friends by this time. Although I disliked the idea of always being constantly referred to as 'Sir', I nevertheless accepted it was an important element of the school's discipline, although I drew the line at corporal punishment, which was still being administered by the Head at that time.

Despite having no personal experience, I was aware, however that people who generally came from either an African, Caribbean or Latin American background, normally possessed natural rhythm when it came to dancing and I quickly recognised this ability amongst many of the boarders. I thus set about organising regular dance competitions in the cavernous area in front of the boys' boarding house. In time these events would attract support amongst the locals, some bringing with them portable music tracks, including hip hop, reggae and blues, that the kids danced along to with spectacular skill and movement. These evenings became highly successful with the kids often insisting that 'Sir' participate fully himself. However, as my future wife would have often observed many years later: "Dancing with you, Bill, is like dancing with Mr Bean!".

We were soon to hear news that the amazing British Aircraft Carrier, HMS Ark Royal, was to make a very brief two-day refuelling stop in Mombasa Harbour. On hearing this, I made contact with the local Harbour Office to enquire if it would be possible for me to take about 50 boarders (from the two boarding houses) on a brief visit to the ship. A few days later I received a message back to say that the Captain had agreed, and a time had been set for an afternoon one-hour visit on its second day in Port.

Derek Bowtell was delighted by this news, yet at the same time expressed surprise that this rare and exceptional authority had been given. Once again, I heard a familiar voice in my head – "If you don't bloody well ask…". When later, sharing this information with the boarders from both houses, uncontrollable pandemonium broke out with unbelievable excitement all round.

Come the day of the visit, like a legion of Regimental Soldiers all lined up, the boarders beautifully turned out in their green and white check school uniforms, made their way up the gang-way steps to what everyone felt was an awesome sight. This enormous craft was simply a mind-blowing experience for everyone. For the next hour, a Lieutenant from the ship's Company, a veritable naval Pied Piper, kindly led us around this majestic craft with many wide-eyed and open-mouthed students in hot pursuit, clinging on to his every word about the ship: its dimensions, the number of aircraft that could be stored in the below deck hangar and on the ship itself, together with a numerous assortment of other facts and figures. Such was the excitement on that day, I suspected few of the boarders got very little sleep that night, heads inevitably filled with memories that would go on to last for a long time.

My second idea, however, did not go quite so smoothly to plan. With Christmas on the horizon, and the school breaking up early in December, Derek asked me if I would kindly produce and direct the school's annual Christmas

Nativity Play to include both boarders as well as other day pupils in the school. I gave a good deal of thought to the upcoming production and by late November had selected my cast of Wise Men, Shepherds, Jesus and Mary. Feeling the production needed a touch of genuine 'realism', I consulted Derek about my idea and although very supportive, he at the same time seemed just a little apprehensive at what I had in mind.

The next day I was on the telephone to the East African Meat Commission (which had a local office based in Mombasa), to enquire as to the possibility of them arranging to loan us a young heifer for our forthcoming school Nativity Play. They asked me to leave the matter with them but assured me that they would get back to me one way or another in the next couple of days. In spite of my reservations, a call came through a few days later to say that they were happy to go ahead and on what day, place and time they were to deliver the small calf to us.

Derek and I were quite taken aback by this news and when I informed the cast, they all embraced the idea very enthusiastically, the Shepherds in particular, who in previous productions had to contend with a stuffed lamb! Many rehearsals followed and by this time the cast of Shepherds knew the key role they would be playing. Come the production day they would bring the small heifer on to the stage whilst the pre-recorded music of 'While Shepherds Watched their Flocks at Night' played in the background on the school's public address system.

On the day of the actual production, a temporary stage had been set up in the front of the school before a packed audience of fellow pupils and teaching staff, including the Head. Members of the cast were full of anticipation and appropriately attired. A few minutes earlier, before the commencement of the production, the heifer had been duly delivered – although considerably bigger than we had envisaged. Undaunted, we tethered it to a rope and handed it over to the principal Shepherd responsible for taking it on to the stage at precisely the right time.

To say the heifer was uncooperative at that time would be a gross understatement. Despite obvious difficulties and the resistance displayed by the heifer, the head Shepherd, accompanied by his two fellow Shepherds, somehow managed to tug and pull the animal on to the centre of the stage at precisely the right time. My thoughts of just how well this was going, combined with the look of wonderment on the audience's faces, witnessing for the very first time a live animal on the stage, were somewhat premature.

Come the time for the Shepherds to exit and to be followed by the Three Kings, accompanied to the music 'We Three Kings of Orient Are', the young heifer obviously had other ideas! Without any warning, it suddenly started to discharge its morning breakfast upon the middle of the stage. Despite the Shepherd's best efforts to get the animal off, it continued discharging a lot more heifer manure. In consequence, Shepherds and Kings were slipping and sliding everywhere!

Soon the music of 'We Three Kings' had come and gone with the Shepherds, assisted by The Kings, still unsuccessfully attempting to pull the animal off the stage. By that time, the audience were howling with undisguised laughter; even the Head was seen to be sniggering. Realising by now that there was no way we were going to rescue the situation, I immediately rushed on to the stage to remove the animal. As I lifted the heavy beast, it continued to deposit yet more hot, steaming manure, but this time down my pristine white shorts and socks and all over my safari boots! This heroic action on my part provoked yet even more hysterical laughter. It was consequently not one of my better days. From then onwards, every time anyone in the school's teaching staff room made a slight reference to the Nativity Play, a lot of hands would invariably cover faces. It was a subject never to be discussed again.

One of my other weekend duties was to manage the football team – not one of my particular skills. The boys had no football boots and had become accustomed, as I did in time, to playing in bare feet. No matter how desperately hard the team's endeavours, games would always conclude with us being given a complete trouncing! However, there would be one notable and memorable exception. One afternoon we played a Muslim School team over their Ramadan Festival. The opposition players were clearly very hungry and thus extremely fatigued, and this gave us one rare opportunity to win the game by one goal! You would have genuinely thought we had just won the Final of the World Cup by the reaction of the boys, who by now had become very accustomed to regularly being on the losing side!

Very early one November day, the local Mombasa 'Daily Nation' newspaper had just been delivered, as it was generally most mornings. The headline was an extraordinarily and a totally unexpected shocking revelation. Global poignant news that consequently touched everyone. 'President Kennedy Assassinated in Texas'. It would become one of those defining moments in one's life, together with the tragic death of Princess Diana many years later, that would remain forever embedded in one's memory. Although the boarders had very little intimate knowledge of the man, they nevertheless knew exactly who he was and what he had come to represent to many people around the globe. As a mark of respect, we collectively bowed our heads in silence and thought before eating breakfast on that exceptionally unforgettable sombre day.

By early December, I had already booked my second-class bus ticket to go back to Nairobi to join Barry and Edwin for the Independence Celebrations, due to take place about ten days later. With only five pounds sterling pocket money to live on each month, a train journey up to Nairobi, wonderful though the thought of it may have been given my memorable earlier experience, was totally out of the question. Ahead, therefore, lay the prospect of a two-day journey by bus, including passing through one of the famous safari parks in Kenya.

It was, to say the least, an unforgettable, and at times, quite traumatic experience and one that I would not have wanted to repeat. The bus was heaving with overloaded luggage on its roof, but also inside were a diverse selection of locals from a wide variety of cultural backgrounds. This included large Kenyan ladies openly breast-feeding their infant child, in addition to several live chickens and other poultry running about uncontrollably and wildly in the bus. I was the only Caucasian on the bus, so I was very much the minority passenger on board.

For the first 50 miles, at both the beginning and end of the road from Mombasa to Nairobi, and vice versa, the surface was tarmacadamed. But approximately 170 miles in-between was what was commonly termed as murrain or mud road. As it had been raining heavily a few days before I left Mombasa, our journey was inevitably punctuated with many hold-ups due to stream-like, large pools of water.

This invariably meant that the bus would, on many occasions, get completely stuck in the mud pools and it was necessary for everyone to vacate the bus until it had freed itself from the quagmire. This was when for the very first time that the expression 'Harambee!' had great significance for me (the Swahili meaning of 'Let's All Pull Together'). We certainly did on several occasions with chants of 'Harambee' being heard many times over the long journey. At one scary breakdown in the late morning, we were situated in the middle of a National Safari Park, yet again pushing the bus. I was convinced that at any moment a pride of lions would descend upon us for early lunch!

By the time we reached Nairobi several hours later, I was feeling very sick and obviously running a fever. The people who met me at the Bus Terminus, including Barry, could see just how ill I looked and immediately rushed me off to a local hospital. Here, I was confined to bed for the next four days and diagnosed with a mild outbreak of malaria, despite always taking my daily anti-malaria pill. Fortuitously, I recovered in time for Barry, Edwin and myself to go to what we expected to be a truly spectacular Independence Celebrations evening, staged at a large arena in Nairobi. Luckily, we had managed to get some very good tickets in advance.

The event fully lived up to our expectations. The early climax to the beginning of the evening, seeing the Union Jack being lowered for the last time and the colourful Kenyan flag, complete with shield and crossed spears, being hoisted, accompanied by the two respective National Anthems played by a Military Band. Witnessing this truly significant event were thousands of spectators in the stadium. Two prominent figures, however, stood out. Jomo Kenyatta, Prime Minister of Kenya, a rather short, stocky man complete with fez hat, depicting the colours of the National Flag and by now with his familiar fly whisk in his hand that he constantly flicked throughout the Ceremony. HRH Prince Phillip, The Duke of Edinburgh, representing the UK Government, looking resplendent in his Royal Naval Admiral of the Fleet Uniform.

The ceremony was followed by wild excitement amongst the very large crowd, although nearby to us were a group of UK ex-pats who looked distinctly unhappy and rather sad. I personally welcomed the fact that the country was now being handed back to its indigenous people who, after all, had lived and occupied the land in the first place.

Next came some extraordinary singing, music and vibrant dancing from the various tribal groups that comprised all the different regions of Kenya, with the exceptionally tall 'Maasai' tribesmen (some over seven feet tall!) stealing the show with their truly energetic, pulsating and thunderous 'Jumping Dance'. All this vigorous activity climaxed with an amazing pyrotechnics display lighting up the dark evening skies. A truly remarkable highlight to an evening that I would remember for many years to come.

Within a few months I had established some very firm relationships with many of the school's teaching staff, including several Indians, local Kenyans and two ex-pats from the UK. To celebrate my 21st birthday in May, they kindly invited me to go for drinks at the very expensive five-star hotel, called Nyali Beach, which would remain a popular destination for holiday tourists for many years to follow. It was a wonderful and memorable occasion, but I was just thankful I wasn't picking up the drinks bill at the end of that evening!

My final remaining months at St. Augustine's School, were virtually 'incident free' and continued to be thoroughly enjoyable for me. The time, however, was rapidly approaching for me to bid my final farewells and inevitably with an exceptionally heavy heart. I had made many good friends amongst the dedicated staff of the school, but more importantly, I had become very emotionally attached to all the kids in the Boarding School with whom I had shared many happy experiences, and whose relentless energy and cheerfulness would be lodged in my memory for many years to come. It was ultimately a tremendous wrench for me to make my final exit and bid them farewell for the very last time and it was extraordinarily difficult holding back the tears.

A significant number of the boarders came from very comfortable backgrounds (children of both Government and Church Ministers). I often wondered for several years afterwards, how many of them would have ultimately go on to establish productive lives for themselves in this newly liberated country. I sincerely hoped that perhaps in some very small way, I may have made a contribution to their ultimate development. Although I would pass through Kenya en-route to Madagascar many times years later, I was never to visit Mombasa again.

It had often been quoted to us during our residential training, prior to going overseas, that we would "get more out of the experience than you could possibly ever hope to contribute". Although somewhat cliched, that very fundamental statement was certainly true of my experience and, I suspected, everyone else who became a volunteer with VSO. This wonderful experience also stirred within me a passion and desire for travel in the future and whenever possible, to enable others to do likewise.

My last couple of days in early August 1964 were spent extremely pleasantly, back again in Nairobi before my eventual flight to Heathrow, visiting one of Kenya's National Parks in the Great Rift Valley, taking this last opportunity to witness the impressive sight of the remaining Pink Flamingos gathered in their thousands on Lake Nakuru.

After the long journey back home, overloaded with many hand-carved wooden animal souvenirs that I had bargained hard for a few days beforehand in Mombasa's Old Port Town market, my family were there to greet me on my return. However, one year on I could see for myself the general decline in my dad's health: he looked grey with a drawn, almost emaciated face. By that time, he had given up full time work and with the support of their local doctor, Mum and Dad were on the point of moving to a small, unfurnished apartment in Reigate, in view of Dad's failing health condition.

Despite virtually a 20-hour flight back, including a two-hour departure delay at Nairobi's Embakasi Airport, and feeling in a physically exhausted state, did not prevent my family from organising a surprise welcome back party at one of the local youth centres with all my family and many friends, including my wonderful former colleague, Irene Taylor.

I took a couple of weeks' rest and relaxation before going to St. Andrew's Home and Club, located in Westminster, to meet the Centre's full time residential Warden, Hugh Dean, before embarking upon an unspecified period of unqualified youth work and another significant change of direction in my life.

Within a few weeks of arriving back home, however, I had a most unexpected letter from Voluntary Service Overseas HQ inviting me, along with other returning volunteers for that year, to a Buckingham Palace reception that was to be hosted by The Queen and The Duke of Edinburgh. This event subsequently turned out to be my second 'brush' with Royalty!

CHANGING DIRECTION

Hugh Dean, together with his wife, Barbara and two young sons, occupied the residential top floor of St. Andrew's Home and Club, located close to the Houses of Parliament. The club comprised a tall, vertical, seven storey building (including the top floor residence) and a designated area on the first floor always referred to as 'the cage' where indoor five-a-side and other activities regularly took place.

It was a most impressive and imposing building, and being a voluntary club, it was very much dependent upon sponsorship and continuous fundraising to keep it running. Nonetheless, it was still regarded as one of the wealthiest clubs in London. It was extremely popular, regularly attracting a very large membership of young people aged between 11 to 21 years of age. The majority of its young people being drawn primarily from a Council House catchment area, Churchill Gardens, Pimlico, just off the main Victoria Street, where many fashionable stores were also located.

With Mum and Dad's imminent move on the horizon, my first priority was to find digs and it was not long before I rented a small but suitably furnished studio flat in an area in South London, Brixton, conveniently located about three miles from the club and ten minutes' ride on the bus and also with an underground station close by. An area that would go on to be a much sought-after neighbourhood.

At the time, Brixton was an area primarily comprising mostly people from an African/Caribbean or Jamaican demographic, post-Windrush generation, who had been encouraged by the Government of the day to settle in the UK, basically to do work that people locally were not interested in undertaking – refuse collection, bus and underground services.

The Sixties were, however, manifestly, a period overshadowed and punctuated by appalling discrimination and racial prejudice and landlords were even allowed to refuse to rent their properties on the basis of a person's ethnic origins or colour of their skin. Over the years, these attitudes, together with much-needed legislation, would bring about fundamental change and resulted eventually in the UK becoming a much more multi-cultural inclusive society.

My attitude and outlook were also very influenced by my mum and dad, who always took the view that 'people were people', irrespective of ethnic origins or religious persuasion, together with a general 'live and let live' view. One exception to that, however, was my dad's patently self-evident view of homosexually at that particular time.

Hugh Dean, the full-time Warden of the club, was a thoroughly professional man who set incredibly exacting standards, but at the same time was an exceptionally hard 'task master' and extremely demanding, and you were certainly expected to give 100% effort in all you did. I soon found myself working almost twelve hours a day, six, and often seven days a week. Somehow, despite this, I knew instinctively that I had the potential to learn a great deal under Hugh's general guidance and that certainly proved to be true.

Not only was I working very long, and often arduous hours, but my monthly pay was half of what I was finally earning when I left my full-time advertising career. I accepted this condition very readily as I had totally made up my mind at this juncture that professional full time Youth Work was my chosen career path.

Similar to my earlier experiences, I was also involved in a host of club activities and events and was specifically given overall responsibility for the under 14s age group section of the club, although still very actively involved with the main age group. The club was extremely well equipped and, unlike many other centres in London, took pride in having its own relatively new 15-seater, rather luxurious mini-bus complete with coloured 'St. Andrew's Home and Club' livery emblazoned down both sides of the vehicle. I was frequently required to drive the bus, taking members to various football games over the weekend or off to some campsite in North Wales or residential centre in High Wycombe, Buckinghamshire.

My involvement with the general mainstream age group of the club, the over 14s, led me to organising two annual Brighton to London sponsored walks to raise money for the club, both events that I took part in personally and completed. Other events included themed disco dance evenings staged in the club's large gym every six months, attracting huge and popular support. Themes such as Halloween – and on one occasion members constructed a life-size Thesaurus Rex with papier-mâché and chicken wire for a Dinosaur themed night.

Another annual event that was very demanding and extremely hard work was 'National Youth Club Week'. This event gave all voluntary clubs and centres throughout the country the opportunity to raise funds for themselves and it was over these periods that I was working virtually non-stop.

Hugh's obsession with perfection knew no bounds, ensuring that the highest possible standards were maintained for the membership, which resulted in a very high degree of respect from both the young people and voluntary staff colleagues who worked in the club. Although many members would refer to him as 'Mr Dean', he was nonetheless very comfortable being called 'Hugh' and never regarded this as being over-familiar in any way.

To broaden my experience, Hugh was concerned that I should learn as much as I could about the club's administration and finances, and this included writing regular reports for the club's Management Committee – duties that ultimately proved to be very beneficial to me.

After a few months at the club, whilst still commuting from my digs in Brixton, my brother-in-law, Ron, offered me the opportunity to buy what he then regarded as his 'pride and joy', a black Ford Popular car (complete with orange manual indicators!) as he and Barbara were moving up to a more modern type of vehicle. I was very flattered that he should give me the first opportunity to buy it and I didn't need to think twice, and we negotiated a mutually acceptable price. This being my first time in life I had owned my very first car. It was like one's first relationship, something never quite forgotten!

The old Popular was put to good use over the coming months and would often be overloaded with boys being transported to the recreational grounds like Clapham Common for football games. Invariably breakdowns would frequently occur en route, resulting in the boys having to push the car for the remainder of the journey!

The car was also something of a social benefit. When I had the very rare evening off, I would arrange a date with a new girlfriend, arriving to pick her up like I was some kind of Formula One driver. The one drawback, however, was that the car had no heating system, so when my female companion for that evening complained about how cold it was, I would respond accordingly: "Don't worry, there is an effective heating system in the car. Me!" The predictable reaction on most occasions meant me returning to my digs earlier than I had planned!

As the car was proving increasingly unpredictable, I would invariably take the train from Victoria to Reigate to visit Mum and Dad as frequently as my busy schedule would allow. It became abundantly clear to me that whilst the comparatively improved air quality in Reigate had brought some benefits to Dad, he remained quite sick, and his deteriorating health became a source of continuing concern for the whole family.

I was very thankful, therefore, that in his last few months, he and I grew quite close to each other.

In spite of his very acute and by now, chronic breathing problems, Dad would, at the conclusion of my day with them, insist on accompanying me back to Reigate's Railway Station, a walk of at least 30 minutes. As a son I may have been a disappointment to him, but those walks together revealed to me just how reassured he was that youth work had become my chosen career path and giving me such personal satisfaction.

In the late spring of 1966, with almost two years under my belt at St. Andrew's, the time had come for me to apply to the National College for the Training of Youth & Community Workers based in Leicester, with Hugh's full support. The College had been established following the publication of a Government Report, 'The Albemarle Report', in 1960, which recommended the expansion of youth and community provision and the need to increase the youth service's professional full-time staff in the country.

With the next college seminar due to commence in September, I applied and was interviewed in Leicester in June of that year. Feeling I had done very well in the personal interviews, I was less confident about my academic performance on the day when required to submit an essay as part of the entry examination.

This legitimate concern became a reality when the Principal, Peter Duke, rang Hugh Dean to say that the College had some genuine concerns as to whether I would be able to cope with the academic demands of the one-year Diploma Course. Although I was never made aware of the contents of the conversation, Margaret, Hugh's dedicated Secretary at the time, told me that she had overheard Hugh tell the Principal over the telephone that: "If they didn't accept Bill Palmer for the course they would be possibly losing one of the finest potential youth workers in the country".

A few days later I was invited back to the College for a personal interview with its Principal, Peter Duke, and to my great relief after a fairly intensive but gentle interview, he confirmed that he was happy to accept me for the upcoming course.

For all the hard and exceptionally long hours of work that he demanded of me over two years, Hugh Dean was a highly principled and loyal person. Had it not been for his timely intervention with the College and his professional observations and support, it would have been highly unlikely that I would have been accepted, and that would have inevitably changed the whole course and direction of my life.

Over my two years at St. Andrew's I had made several friends amongst the voluntary colleagues who had worked there and also established excellent relationships with many members of the club. A few days before my departure I traded in my old Ford Popular car for a relatively newish second-hand Mini car. This purchase would not have been possible had it not been for the Management Committee of the club who presented me with an extraordinarily generous cheque as acknowledgement of my work over the previous two years, but also in recognition that I had been paid a relatively modest salary over that period.

It was, again, with a very heavy heart, as with my Kenyan experience two years earlier, that I left St. Andrew's but having learned a great deal under Hugh's careful guidance and tutelage. My next move would be another uncertain chapter in my life, yet I was still a relatively young 23-year-old.

Twin sister Pam

INTELLIGENTLY OBJECTIVE, NOT EMOTIONALLY INVOLVED

A month before heading up to Leicester, I had already given notice to the owner of my digs in Brixton, having thoroughly enjoyed becoming part of what had developed into principally an Afro-Caribbean district, complete with its intoxicating and vibrant atmosphere.

By late July, I had received a letter from the College confirming that with 15 other male students, I would be a full-time resident at a place called Knighton Lodge – a very large three-floored Victorian House that had been suitably converted as a residential block. The Lodge was approximately five miles from the actual College building, but daily transport would be provided for each day's return journey. The Lodge itself was set in a very leafy suburb of Leicester and thus enjoyed a somewhat quiet and tranquil atmosphere, highly appropriate for the forthcoming year of intensive academic study.

Accompanying the letter was also a list of recommended reading that would be required to be undertaken before the commencement of the course. Most of the reading matter concerned the History of Youth and Community Services, both nationally and overseas, numerous legal Government Legislations, covering various developments over two centuries. But I was also surprised to find that some relatively 'light' reading had also been included on the list. Stan Barstow's 'A Kind of Loving' was one I particularly enjoyed with the principal theme of the book about a working-class man caught up in an unhappy marriage. Something that would resonate very strongly with me much later on in my life.

I fell in love with Knighton Lodge immediately upon arrival and this initial feeling remained with me throughout the coming year. The 14 other male students who were also resident with me bonded from day one and we were therefore to go on to develop very close and supportive relationships.

The College itself was virtually a collection of several wooden linked buildings (almost resembling outdoor classrooms in schools), clustered together over quite a large area surrounded by a mixture of both very pleasant deciduous and evergreen trees with grassed areas and playing fields in the distance. The College had numerous small tutorial rooms, a large lecture hall, activity areas, a very well stocked library and small multi-faith chapel and a huge refectory where the College's 100 students and approximately 20 staff could be accommodated to enjoy daily lunch together.

There were ten tutorial groups with ten students in each group. Our tutor, Miss Joy Stallard, was a fairly elderly spinster in her mid-sixties but clearly a highly experienced practitioner as well as academic. She would become one of the most supportive, kind and caring tutors you would have chosen yourself if you had been given the opportunity. I felt she had been specifically selected to tutor our group, given her nature and personality, as I suspected our group had been drawn together on the basis of being regarded as less academically gifted. Throughout our year's study we would always address her as 'Miss Stallard'.

Our mixed gender tutorial group was drawn from a variety of different backgrounds, including ethnic and multi-faith groupings; a Jamaican man, a woman from South Africa and two Jewish people. All these students, identical to my experience at Knighton Lodge, would also go on to share very close relationships with me over our one year together.

Three tutorial discussion groups formed part of our regular weekly schedule including frequent assignments; 500-word essays that needed to be handed in the following week. Initially, I struggled with the academic demands of the course, but during personal tutorial interviews, Joy always gave me the utmost of encouragement. Although there were times when I felt my essay assignment fell short of what had been expected, Joy would correct some of my grammar and content but would always leave a supportive note telling me that I was improving and to keep up the good progress.

Her constant support and kindness to all of her students ensured that we grew each week in confidence. On a personal level I fully embraced all the academic side to the course, and it was especially rewarding when later in the year, I was given a B+ for a 5000-word dissertation on the 'History of Voluntary Youth Work in the UK'.

Twice a week, all students would be expected to join lectures (often with distinguished visiting speakers), covering myriad subjects: Law, History of Youth & Community Services, Political Developments, and many areas concerned with Social Welfare in general. These one-hour lectures were invariably followed by individual tutorial groups, to discuss in more depth the implications of the talk that had just been presented.

Thankfully, it was not all study and no play at Leicester College. We were offered a host of activities to participate in, given our future Youth Work careers, three of which had to be compulsory activities. Predictably, I chose Drama as one of my subjects, but also decided to opt for two new activities I had never participated in before: fencing and horse riding.

I had little difficulty settling into the Drama group and eventually participated in a play that was presented towards the end of the course to fellow students and staff in the large lecture hall. Fencing, however, was quite challenging for me, and there were not that many occasions when I could shout *'touché'*, but I fenced on regardless.

I will never quite forget, however, my initial reaction to our first visit to the nearby stables. The horses were already assembled for us to mount and the seven students and myself taking part already kitted up in suitable attire, including hard hat. When first introduced to my selected 'steed', a veritable giant of a horse with goodness knows how many hands high in stature, I took a very sharp intake of breath. Even given my lofty height, I began to wonder just how I would mount such a 'titan' without the assistance of a small step ladder.

"Come on, get on it, 'Flossie's' a very sweet natured, gentle soul," I was reassured by the stable lad, who by now was helping to lift me over this mass of 'equine' anatomy. No sooner had I sat on the saddle and placed my feet in the stirrups, when suddenly 'Flossie' (good natured, or otherwise), was off without any warning or encouragement from me, trotting furiously like some kind of steeple chaser! Unlike Dad's favourite, I was no Lester Piggott Champion Jockey Rider! My remaining outings to the stables were never quite as eventful as this first experience. By that time, I had been permanently assigned to a horse virtually the size of a pony. But I never complained.

I was also pressured by other college friends to take an active part in the College Rugby team; a totally new experience for me. Despite my reluctance, it was not too long before I found myself donning the team's maroon and yellow rugby shirt and allotted the wing position. It would never become one of my most favourite activities despite enjoying the spirit of camaraderie that existed within the team. I was nonetheless regarded as a modestly good winger with some speed, except as the Captain of the team would often observe: "You would be so good, given your swift-like runs up the wing, if only, Bill, you would remember to take the ball with you!".

In addition to all the College activity, we were also assigned two, one-month field youth work placements that were monitored and assessed as part of the course curriculum. My first was in West London and my second in Bath, Somerset, two youth work assignments that I thoroughly enjoyed, especially the two households who had accommodated me.

On my twenty-fourth birthday during late May 1967, I had a very intimate evening dinner with a stunningly beautiful young woman, Anne, whom I had met several months earlier at a party and fallen head over heels in love with and we subsequently got engaged that evening. Anne, who originally hailed from Hull, shared a flat with a girlfriend and worked in a local branch of a National Insurance Company in Leicester. Over time, however, the relationship began to struggle and eventually we agreed to break off the engagement on amicable terms; Anne being the first 'love' of my life.

We were now just a matter of weeks away from the conclusion of the course and no student really knew for certain at that stage if they had passed the College course successfully, or not. To our collective relief, a few days later we all received a letter of congratulations from Principal Peter Duke, informing us that we had passed and would be awarded our Diploma at a Graduation passing out ceremony event before we finally broke up. It was a year when all participating students had passed the course. The sense of joy around the corridors of the College and also Knighton Lodge was unmistakable!

Despite all the personal challenges, especially the rigorous academic demands, I thoroughly enjoyed my one-year in Leicester and found the more theoretical aspects of the course as equally fulfilling and rewarding. The constant reminder and emphasis throughout that year reinforced with being

'Intelligently objective and not emotionally involved', would remain with me, although in reality I would still find it difficult sometimes to put into practice.

With the conclusion of the course in sight, the College Library had doubled-up as a general staff recruitment area with notice boards advertising various Youth and Community vacant appointments around the country.

However, I had already been approached by Paul Reed, who had taken over as Warden back at St. Andrew's in Westminster, London, following Hugh Dean's departure to take up a senior post within the Prison Service. Apparently, Paul had heard of my reputation and was anxious to have me back as his full-time Deputy on a qualified Youth Worker's salary. After much deliberation to his proposal, I agreed with the caveat that I only serve about a year as I was anxious to have the opportunity of running my own centre. Paul accepted this, and thus my immediate future was relatively secure.

Part of the rationale for this decision was heavily influenced by the fact that Mum and Dad lived not too far away, and I could continue to make regular visits. This was especially important to me as Mum's most recent letter had set alarm bells ringing about Dad's continuing ill-health.

In common with other students, receiving my Youth and Community Diploma on Graduation Day was indeed a very proud moment in my life. I would particularly remember seeing in the distance on that special ceremony day in late July, our very supportive personal tutor throughout that challenging year, Miss Stallard, beaming characteristically with 'Joy'.

"IF YOU DON'T BLOODY WELL ASK!"

Again, I was able to secure some digs locally near the Elephant and Castle, a short bus and tube journey to Westminster. Paul Reed was a delightful man but fully appreciated that my time with the club would inevitably be short-lived. Within a brief time, I had returned to many of the familiar activities that had engaged me fully back in Hugh's former days. In contrast, Paul had a much more relaxed attitude and style to the Centre and its running, but was still very effective professionally, and extremely popular both in the club and with residents of the surrounding area.

Leaving the club quite late one evening to make my way over Parliament Square to catch my bus back to my digs in Elephant and Castle, I had a somewhat bizarre encounter. A very well spoken, quite tall gentleman with a brown Trilby hat, a prominent characteristic of a man I recognised immediately as Jeremy Thorpe, the Leader of the Liberal party. He engaged me in a brief conversation and eventually invited me back to his nearby apartment for a drink. An invitation I politely declined as I was anxious to catch my bus. Many years later,

Jeremy Thorpe would be involved in a highly controversial relationship with a young man, leading to a sensational court case and accusation of attempted murder of this young man. Although acquitted, his professional reputation was, however, very damaged. Many years later I often wondered what may have happened had I accepted that invitation!

Paul was a very kind, generous and a charming man and following a year back in the club he fully supported me in my endeavours to find a vacant youth centre post. Following a couple of unsuccessful applications, I finally got my first big break. A major new Voluntary Youth Work Project, with a £350,000 youth centre building, still under construction, was advertised in the 'Times Educational Supplement'. It was the full-time post of Manager of a centre to be named 'Colchester Youth House' with a new building located just off the main High Street, situated in a residential area of the town called the 'Dutch Quarter'.

The project was an entirely voluntary one with all the fundraising for the building and future running costs being raised locally and from national youth charities. Essex County Council, the Local Education Authority, however, had agreed to make its contribution by employing the Manager as a full-time Statutory Worker of the County Council. This would ensure, therefore, that the person appointed could take full advantage of all the benefits and security of a Local Authority worker, including the excellent Teachers' Pension Scheme.

I was absolutely enthralled by what I had read about the project and decided that in spite of my relatively young years, combined with my limited practical experience, I would apply, hearing once again that unmistakeable voice of my dad in my head, "If you don't bloody well ask...!" So off went my application.

By early September 1968, I received a letter from a Mrs Blaxill, the Chairman, informing me that I had been short-listed, along with ten other candidates for the post of Manager and was being invited for interview two weeks later in mid-September. It further stated that each candidate would be individually escorted, at different times, in the morning around the yet to be completed Youth House building in the Dutch Quarter with the main interviews taking place at the beginning of the afternoon in the Town Hall in the High Street.

Paul and I both shared a combined feeling of anticipation and excitement. Nevertheless, Paul wisely cautioned that as this was obviously a very large project in Essex with the support of the Local Authority, together with what he felt would be a strong field of candidates, I should seriously consider lowering my expectations, although that did not stop me thinking about all the potential possibilities of such an opportunity.

Over the next few weeks, I did a great deal of thinking and additional study, both about Colchester and its history, and Paul agreed to conduct a few role-play interviews with me so that he could make some observations and constructive comments. "Show your commitment and obvious passion, Bill, but try to follow whenever possible the 'kiss' principle: 'Keep it Short and Simple'. You don't have to be abrupt with your responses but avoid the temptation of going on too long." These were wise words from Paul who by now I had come to respect and admire greatly.

I received a follow-up letter from the Chairman confirming that I had been booked into the George Hotel in the town's High Street the night before the day of the interviews and my visit to the Youth House construction site confirmed for 11.30 the following morning. Thus, in mid–September, I arrived in Colchester for my overnight stay and, somehow, I instinctively felt at home, which I took to be a good omen at that time. The George Hotel was considered to be the most iconic and oldest hotel in the area, and it certainly lived up to that reputation.

The following morning, I met at the construction site a fairly elderly, grey-haired man who introduced himself as Gordon Kent, who was an accountant by profession. He was the Treasurer of the new Youth House Project. A most engaging man who chatted away about the origins of the project whilst escorting me around what was a truly amazing building with many outstanding architectural features. It was quite apparent that no expense had been spared to make this one of the most impressive youth projects, not just in the County of Essex, but perhaps the whole country.

Before I left Gordon for my afternoon interview, he gave me one final piece of advice: "Bill, if you are really serious about getting this post, and your commitment has certainly impressed me, make sure you get on the right side of the Chairman, Mrs Eileen Blaxill. Believe me when I say she is the driving force and the powerhouse behind this project. Good luck, Bill!"

Colchester's Town Hall was a rather ornate and very historical place and by 2pm all ten candidates had gathered in an ante-

"IF YOU DON'T BLOODY WELL ASK!"

room, just off a large assembly room where the interviews themselves were due to take place. Earlier conversations had revealed just how experienced most of the other candidates were and therefore I was not fully confident at that stage I would be in contention. However, I was determined to give it my best shot and Paul's advice of 'kiss' was uppermost in my mind.

It was quite late, around five o'clock, that just one other candidate and I were left waiting to be called. Eventually the large wooden assembly door opened, and I was invited to enter, but immediately taken by complete surprise. What confronted me was a very large circular table around which were seated about 12 people, predominately male, except for one very elegantly dressed and quite distinguished, elderly, grey-haired lady who sat at the top of the table. It was patently obvious to me straight away that this was the Chairman, the formidable Mrs Blaxill I had heard about previously.

The interviewing panel comprised people drawn from the County, Borough, Area Youth Office as well as four additional members from the Youth House's Management Committee. In reality, it represented the largest number of people I had ever been interviewed by before.

I was being quizzed throughout with vigorous questioning, but somehow, I managed to keep my composure, making it clear my total commitment to equal opportunities and to the principle of young people's empowerment and that these were the underlying values and practice guiding my thinking, and as such a central tenet to my youth work beliefs.

It was precisely at that very moment that I caught Eileen Blaxill's eye and reassuring smile, and somehow instinctively knew that, as far as she was concerned, I was exactly who she had in mind for this challenging post.

Less than an hour later, I was invited back into the room and offered the position of Manager and it was mutually agreed that I would start my new post at the beginning of the New Year 1969, along with a quite generous starting salary.

Everybody back at the club, especially Paul, were thrilled by my appointment, but any premature celebrations would soon be promptly overshadowed. I was visiting Mum and Dad at the weekend, following my successful interview, to share with them my joy and excitement over my appointment. However, when I arrived by car at their flat in Reigate on the Saturday morning, Mum was looking exceedingly anxious and stressed and was waiting for an ambulance to arrive to take Dad to the local hospital, following an apparent collapse a few minutes earlier. Soon the ambulance had arrived, and Dad was quickly wheeled out by the paramedics with Mum accompanying him, and me following by car. Mum was to tell me later that once in the ambulance, the paramedics began to immediately start resuscitating Dad.

Due to heavy traffic on that day, I was unable to keep up with the ambulance, although fortunately knew exactly where the hospital was located. About 20 minutes later I arrived at the Accident and Emergency section only to be informed that Dad had already been taken to the Intensive Care Unit. I immediately took a lift up to the appropriate floor where Dad was being treated, but advised that I could not enter at that point as he was still receiving emergency treatment by the doctors.

It seemed like a lifetime before Mum eventually appeared before me, but the expression on her face and furrowed forehead told me everything I needed to know. "Your dad's gone," she said quietly.

Totally shocked by this unexpected turn of events, Mum asked me if I wanted to see Dad alone before he was taken away to the morgue. I walked very slowly to the actual bedside where he was located and drew back the curtains surrounding his bed. Lying there outstretched in a pair of hospital pyjamas was my dad, looking for all the world as if he were taking one of his frequent naps that he often indulged in during those latter few months in Reigate. What was cruelly ironic, but purely unintentional with his ultimate destination to the morgue, was that one of the nursing staff had already attached a brown luggage-type label to the big toe of his left foot that simply read 'Palmer'.

To me he was not just 'Palmer'. He was my dad. And for all his faults, he would always remain a thoroughly decent, honourable man with immense personal courage and integrity that I had witnessed many times throughout his relatively short life. He was a staunchly proud family man who would go to any length to defend and protect his family and, as far as I was concerned, that marked him out as a very special person.

For all the disappointment he may have occasionally felt about me, he was nevertheless my dad and I loved him, and his home-spun philosophy "If you don't bloody well ask!"

had inspired me many times. It was extremely hard at that moment to fully comprehend that my dad, a man still in his early fifties, had already been taken from us. I could instinctively feel myself beginning to well up, but somehow knowing how masculinity meant so much to him personally, managed to contain, with great difficulty, my emotions. I remember thinking to myself that if I were ever to have a son, I would ensure he knew it was perfectly normal to cry and it was okay to show your emotional feelings.

The impact of Dad's death on Mum was self-evident. For all the trials and tribulations of their marriage – Dad's epileptic fits, mood swings, long periods of unemployment, gambling and smoking addictions – Mum clearly loved him very much and had made the ultimate sacrifice when she demonstrated this very early on in their relationship by getting married to him, much against her own parents' wishes.

Dad's death would also go on to have a profound effect upon the whole family, but most especially my elder sister, Barbara. She was very distressed by the news of his premature death. They had shared a very close relationship over his brief lifetime. Dad would always continue from then onwards to have a very special place in Barbara's heart.

Dad's untimely death was somewhat paradoxical given the longevity of his own parents, our grandmother and grandfather, living well into their mid-nineties. I always remember, in particular, how Grandfather had a regular habit of taking snuff and always seeing the mustard-like stains under the bridge of his nose or down one of his favourite waistcoats that were a familiar accessory.

A week later Dad was cremated at the Surrey & Sussex Crematorium; a place that would become somewhat symbolic to us as a family.

Friends and colleagues alike were saddened by news of my dad's sudden death. However, for me, a new beginning lay ahead and a fresh chapter in my life beckoned. After serving out my remaining months' notice at St. Andrew's, I was finally off to the Garrison and Historical Civil War Town of Colchester. Another door opening to what was an uncertain, but nevertheless, potentially exciting future.

Just one final thought lingered in my head as I made my journey up to the Anglian region. I wished my dad had lived long enough for me to tell him my news about my Manager's appointment in Colchester. Somehow, I feel he would have been very pleased, maybe even a little proud.

SKINHEADS AND 'BOVVER' BOOTS!

In the late autumn I visited Colchester for two days, staying in a local hotel and to use the opportunity to seek out personal future accommodation as well as having a general get-together with the Chairman of the centre, Eileen Blaxill.

Although it was a particularly cold month when I visited, it nevertheless confirmed my initial impressions that Colchester was a delightful town, with its long High Street, full of quaint individual shops and coffee bars, dominated by its long history of Civil War conflicts during the 17th century – some buildings still bearing the signs of cannon fire holes on their walls. Towards the foot of the High Street stood an impressive Norman Castle, complete with moat, that was now functioning as a very popular museum. Paradoxically, in so many ways, London was the total opposite, with its almost 24/7 buzz that I had come to adopt and love, yet somehow, I already felt extremely relaxed about what was to become my permanent surroundings for the next few years.

I had already been given, in advance, the name of a contact regarding accommodation in the town, Mrs Joy Donnelly, who I was to discover to be an incredibly entrepreneurial person, as well as a very astute property developer. Joy lived with her husband, a local solicitor, and teenage daughter and son in a large house in the picturesque area called the Dutch Quarter, situated just off the main High Street, and adjacent to the Youth House site.

Apparently, many of these original dilapidated Dutch cottages had fallen into a state of disrepair along with the area and were consequently being sold very cheaply. Joy immediately saw a unique opportunity, and over a number of years purchased more than 20 of these properties, modernised them and furnished them with a mixture of modern and ancient furniture (much of which she had bid for at local auctions). Once furnished, she rented these to local university students and young professionals at quite moderate rents, thus the area gained a somewhat 'renaissance' reputation as a community environment comprising these kinds of individuals.

When Joy and I met for the first time, she confessed that she had been one of several vocal critics opposing the building of a new Youth House. Yet in spite of meeting for the first time, the very individual who was going to run the project, in no way did that affect her attitude toward me.

Joy proceeded to show me an elegantly converted fully furnished studio cottage flat, a stone's throw away from the Youth House building, which I accepted immediately. This was not only going to be a very comfortable place to live and also within my financial budget, but more importantly, a relief to know that my immediate accommodation problem had been resolved.

As Joy and I made our way back from the cottage we passed a fairly large, modern and quite sophisticated building set back from the road. When I enquired as to its use, Joy promptly replied, "That's the 'Andromeda' Night Club, an Adult Only Social Club, which is very popular in the town and extremely well run by its owner. You must find some time to visit as I am sure you will enjoy it." Only to discover later that the owner of the nightclub was also one of the objectors to the project. But the Andromeda would soon come to feature quite strongly in my social life.

Eileen Blaxill was a person who very much displayed her 'Conservative' credentials on her sleeve, but there was no mistaking her total commitment to the young people of the town. She had been the primary driving force behind the establishment of the Youth House and over several years had raised thousands of pounds. Eileen's husband was Chairman and Managing Director of the largest DIY store in the region; consequently, she was financially very comfortable, living in a very large Victorian-styled house with substantial grounds, located north of the town centre.

It was here that she had invited me over for lunch and I was slightly astonished to find our meal served by a rather elderly lady 'retainer' she referred to as her permanent help. Over lunch Eileen and I chatted, and it was soon very clear that we had virtually identical views about the general philosophy and direction that the Youth House would take. Eileen was particularly impressed by my undoubted commitment to the empowerment of young people, something that she also felt very resolute about. It was at that stage she informed me about the existence of a relatively large Steering Group of Young Adults (mostly aged from age 18 years upwards). The group had already been established with a view to working alongside the newly appointed Manager of the project in shaping its future, and Eileen agreed to set up a meeting with this group once I had settled into the town a few weeks later.

During our conversation, Eileen also informed me that the President of the new Youth House was Mr Anthony Buck, then Colchester's local Member of Parliament (who would eventually become Lord Buck after being awarded a Peerage during Margaret Thatcher's time as Prime Minister). Later I was to find Anthony, who always insisted on being addressed as 'Tony', to be an incredibly energetic man with a most dynamic personality and very popular with his local constituents. Anthony and Eileen were not only two of the strongest supporters of the project but would in the future be very supportive to me, personally.

At the beginning of the year, having settled in, one of my first appointments was an interview with a journalist from the local rag, 'The Colchester Express'. It developed into quite a long session with me sharing all my thoughts, ideas and general philosophy about how I saw the Youth House operating. That week, on one of the inside pages of the paper, a full page had been devoted entirely to the interview with the headline: "Young Manager for 'Teenyboppers' Youth House", accompanied by a photograph of me posing outside the yet to be completed Youth House. It was a slightly misleading headline, but more importantly, the article generated a good deal of widespread publicity.

In this first week, I also met on site the centre's architect, and it was immediately evident that he was very committed to ensuring that the architectural brief reflected the ideals, modernity and ambitions of the centre. He took me through the various stages of building development and also confirmed that if all should go according to plan, the building would be completed by the early summer, hopefully the month of July. It was at that point I began to appreciate the enormity of the project and the ultimate responsibility this challenging project presented.

With no office at that time, the local Area Youth Officer, Barney Carlton, graciously offered some space with telephone in his office that he was prepared to share with me over the coming months until the completion of my own office in the new building. This gesture was typical of a man who would become yet another very important role model in my life. Throughout my tenure, Barney would always be ever on hand to support and give me good professional advice, and I consequently developed a very close relationship with him, together with his wonderful French wife, Jackie.

A good deal of my time in the office as part of my early preparation, included selecting the various materials and patterns for the curtains and carpets within the youth house and the daunting task of selecting a comprehensive range of equipment for the various activity areas as well as furniture for the whole centre, including the main social-cum-coffee bar area that would ultimately become the epicentre of the centre. Given its voluntary status, the Management Committee had, nevertheless, still allocated a very generous budget which allowed me to purchase some exceptionally well-designed furniture that I hoped would create an environment of quality and reinforce a strong sense of belonging and ownership by the future membership of the centre.

A few evenings later I met with the centre's Youth Steering Group, a collection of about 20 young men and women from about the age of 18 upwards, with two who were over 21, many of whom I felt were drawn from comfortable middle-class backgrounds.

They were a most enthusiastic and committed group and I spent the evening sharing with them thoughts about my general plans and aspirations for the Youth House which were very well received. Over the coming months, the Centre Youth Steering Committee would also come to play a pivotal role during the first few months of operation of the Centre, taking many of the important decisions governing the centre and me using them as an important conduit to channel new ideas and thoughts.

One female member of the Steering Group who was 19 at the time and on the verge of going off to university in Norwich, particularly caught my eye. Isobel was a rather demure, beautiful young woman with short brunette hair and dark brown eyes and devastating smile, together with a delightful and caring personality. She also came from a very comfortable background, her father being the Chief Executive of a large Engineering Company in the region.

Over the next 18 months Isobel and I would share a very intimate relationship with me making several weekend visits to see her at university, and after a year we announced our engagement: my second fiancée in life! Once again, however, the constant pressure of my visits to her in Norwich, together with the enormous demands of the Youth House began taking its toll on me and sadly after two years we mutually agreed to part company. This was the second relationship breakdown in my life, and I started to question quite seriously, for the first time my own sexuality, but quickly dismissed any seeds of doubt I may have had as purely transient.

By late June, owing to some very unexpected inclement weather, including heavy snow falls in February, had led inevitably to building delays with the architect informing the Management Committee that the completion date had now had to be put back to the beginning of September.

To compensate for this disappointing news, Eileen shared with us all that the Lord Lieutenant of Essex, Sir John Ruggles-Brise, had just informed her earlier that Princess Anne had responded positively to our invitation to 'Officially' open the Youth House and a date had been set for the beginning of October (this was also to be her first 'Royal Engagement' at the age of 18). This announcement was met with much excitement and for me personally, a further opportunity to become acquainted with yet another member of the 'Windsor' family.

Over the coming weeks, invitations were going out to dignitaries that were regarded as the 'Great and the Good', VIPs and general 'hoi polloi' from all parts of the town and region. By that time the Youth Steering Committee number had swelled to more than 50, providing sufficient numbers of young people in the Youth House come the day of the Royal visit.

A few days later, a special meeting was convened at Eileen's house in the morning between the Chief Executive of Essex County Council, MP Anthony Buck, Eileen and me to discuss outline plans for the day of the Royal visit. After a few pleasantries and coffee, the Chief Executive shared his plans for the forthcoming visit with the emphasis very much on the dignitaries, and the young people of the centre relegated to a back seat. I plucked up sufficient courage to say that I felt the young people should play the prominent role on the day and that the Chairman of the Young People's Steering Group, Richard Ward, along with the Chairman, Mrs Blaxill, should give a welcome speech to the Princess. Emboldened, I further suggested that the young people and myself should escort HRH around the centre, introducing her to staff members and the various activity areas and then ten of the young people take afternoon tea with her. Once tea had finished, Mrs Blaxill and Mr Buck could join them and escort the Princess to where she could unveil a commemorative plaque and then be led to the final line up of dignitaries to bid her farewell. Mrs Blaxill and Mr Buck could then escort the Princess out of the centre and down the passageway to her waiting Bentley car. In the meantime, I could have all the young people assembled on the balcony, overlooking the street, where they could wave goodbye to Her Royal Highness.

The embarrassing library silence that followed my proposals were suddenly broken by both Eileen and Anthony who said, almost in unison, "Bill's absolutely right! This is exactly how the day should be organised with the young people of the Youth House playing the key roles. We couldn't agree more and fully support Bill's plans".

Whatever the expression on the Chief Executive's face might have been, he finally responded: "Well, it's certainly unorthodox to say the very least and not the usual pattern we normally follow on these Royal visits, but if both the President and Chairman are content with Mr Palmer's suggested alternatives then so be it, we will go ahead on that basis". It was very reassuring for me, given my relatively short time with the Youth House, knowing that I could now come to rely on both Eileen and Anthony's full support.

Over the next few weeks, with most of the building completed, it was a general hive of activity around the centre with caterers being organised, seat arrangements allocated, portable stage ordered, including a selection of very large pot plants that were to be strategically placed around the centre together with oil paintings from local galleries and exhibited on the various centre walls – this was all being undertaken to generally enhance what was already a very sophisticated environment. It had also already been agreed by the Youth House's Management Committee and Steering Group of Young People that the formal opening of the centre would now take place following the 'official' Royal Opening, at the beginning of October.

I was absolutely delighted for Eileen as she had worked tirelessly for many years to see this dream of hers become a reality, and the forthcoming Royal visit by Princess Anne was certainly the icing on the cake. Eileen could hardly contain her excitement and talked enthusiastically about her planned visit to London to get a suitable and, I suspected, very expensive outfit, for the occasion.

It had also been agreed that my mum should be invited to the official opening ceremony which pleased me no end. I also ensured that two of the most vocal critics of the project, Joy Donnelly and the Manager of the Andromeda Night Club, were also invited and I was grateful that they both accepted the invitation.

As the day approached there was an unmistakable atmosphere of excitement in the town, especially amongst the young people who were now going to play a major role on the day of the visit itself. The Gods were certainly with us on that day in early October, it being a beautifully glorious sunny day. The young Royal Highness looked most elegant dressed in a vivid orange outfit complete with matching hat as she stepped out of her Royal Bentley car at Colchester's Youth House.

All the arrangements, barring a few nervous moments, went off according to plan, with the Princess being very charming throughout the visit. The conclusion, and in many ways the highlight of the day, was seeing Princess Anne looking up smilingly and waving at the assembled group of young people who had by now gathered on the balcony as she stepped back into her car. It seemed to us that Princess Anne, on her first official Royal Engagement, had really enjoyed her time with

UP, DOWN AND OUT!

the young people who had played such an integral role on the day itself. It was also a relief for me, as the Chief Executive of Essex County Council before his departure, came to me to thank me personally for what he had felt had been an extraordinarily successful day. I also knew that my mum had been very proud of me on that day.

That evening, Princess Anne's visit featured very prominently on Anglian Television News and coverage dominated most of the local newspapers with several pages devoted to pictures taken during the Royal 'walkabout'.

Once the euphoria was over, it was time to get down to the real business in hand, the 'formal' opening of the centre itself. I had by that time recruited a very talented group of part-time paid staff, including the appointment of a receptionist to welcome the young people as they entered the centre. Additionally, I also recruited a large army of volunteers to staff the coffee-bar.

Extensive advertising had already been undertaken prior to the opening, with me spending several days touring local secondary schools and the local college getting the message out about the opening night and the kind of facilities they could expect to enjoy and conditions of membership. When addressing school pupils, I particularly emphasised the crucial role members would play in the decision-making processes and this general theme seemed to be very well received.

Come the scheduled opening night at 7:00pm all the staff were in attendance for this opening launch. Part-time paid and volunteers, as well as members of the Young Peoples

Steering Group with myself, were already gathered together in the centre by 6:45pm.

The atmosphere was a mixture of excitement, anticipation and to some extent, apprehension. We were all beginning to contemplate whether or not the previous weeks' intensive promotion efforts had paid off. We did not have to wait long before getting our answer. In the background from the alleyway that led to the four glass entrance main opening doors, a distant rumble could be distinctly heard increasing in volume and strength and portent of an on-coming catastrophic human tsunami!

Suddenly, we could all see for ourselves through the long exterior glass windows in the centre's coffee bar, what resembled a veritable regimental army. Over one hundred of a group identified as 'Skinheads' and renowned for violence, complete with 'bovver boots' (known as Doc Marten's), tattoos, shaven heads and body piecings, both male and female, along with loud chants of "E'er we go! E'er we go!" accompanied by dozens of clenched fists being punched into the air, drawn inextricably to the entrance doors like a powerful magnet.

At that moment in time, several chins hit the deck, my own included, and everyone was on tenterhooks. The sensitive, but obviously very nervous female receptionist, who by now was looking at dozens of skinhead faces pressed hard up against the main door windows, looked to me and said quietly, "Bill, what should we do?" My answer was prompt and unequivocal: "They have as much right to be here as anyone else, so let them in".

Most of the group had come from a social housing development area called 'Greenfields', a Council house estate some four miles north of the town, so they had obviously made some effort to get to the Youth House. Undaunted, we slowly and gradually took names and a small cover charge for that evening, The Steering Youth Committee having already decided in advance that potential members should be given a guest period time of two weeks before taking out full membership, giving them the opportunity to see whether the centre was for them or not. A system I felt eminently sensible.

Within 30 minutes this group were literally clamouring all over the centre, exploring every nook and cranny, to the consternation of some of the staff who were still nevertheless doing their level best to engage with them. By this time the Young Peoples Working Group had become somewhat agitated by this invasion and a small delegation approached me to express their concerns, feeling that this particular group would not in their view fit into the general ethos of the Youth House. In response, I made it clear that as far as I was concerned that these young 'so-called' skinheads, many of whom I felt coming from quite disadvantaged backgrounds, had as much right to be members of the centre as anyone else, providing they accepted the basic rules of respecting other users as well as the Youth House environment. In spite of these genuinely held concerns, the group remained staunchly supportive to both the Youth House and me.

With the building now 'heaving' with upwards of 200 young people, including other young people who had also come along, there was already an unmistakable air of tension and this atmosphere would prevail for some time to come. The

SKINHEADS AND 'BOVVER' BOOTS!

message was clearly communicated to all the membership, however, and most especially the skinhead faction, that any offending behaviour would ultimately result in suspension from the centre. Staff were also reminded that maintaining 'boundaries' were key to ensuring a harmonious and safe environment for all.

Soon a varied programme of activities was beginning to bed down, including a very popular and successful disco dance every Friday evening, attracting over 200 young people and held in the centre's basement. Whilst an uneasy atmosphere continued, potential incidents were rapidly defused and resolved by an increasingly experienced staff team. These early formative days were, for both the staff and me, very challenging, but Barney, the Area Youth Officer, was always there to give encouragement and support, including several staff training sessions that he organised.

As a voluntary centre dependent on constant fundraising, when an offer was made by a contact in the local College (where I had already enrolled for a drama group), that a popular and well-known musical group, 'East of Eden', were prepared to stage a 'gig' at the Youth House two months ahead and give their services free, it was an offer I simply could not turn down. Unbeknown to me at that time, this was going to be, in youth work terms, my first real 'Baptism of Fire!'. Over the coming weeks preparations were put in hand with a good deal of publicity circulated locally, including an article in the press.

The response was beyond all our expectations and come the evening, literally hundreds were queuing in the alleyway adjacent to the centre. With a cover charge of £3, this had all the hallmarks of being a spectacular fundraising event, as well as a memorable evening. It would certainly become the latter. The East of Eden group were already on stage and well into their second musical number and at that point over 400 young people had gathered in the main hall swinging and singing along, the coffee bar especially doing a roaring trade. For me at that stage of the evening, it couldn't get any better!

My premature optimism, however, was quickly shaken when a member of staff alerted me to a small minority of the skinhead cohort looking the worse for drink and displaying menacing behaviour. During East of Eden's third number the situation had escalated, and this minority had begun systematically head-butting anyone in their path, especially those they considered to be college 'geek' types. No matter the best efforts by the staff to control and prevent yet more unprovoked attacks, many people were by that time leaving the centre in droves. Meanwhile, East of Eden had abandoned the stage, taking their instruments to seek 'refuge' in my office.

The situation had deteriorated so badly that for the first time since our opening, we were left with no other option other than to call the police to help resolve this totally out of control scene and a general ratcheting up of tension all round. Eventually the situation was finally brought under control with the police making a number of arrests amongst the minority offending group who had caused this very disruptive 'fracas'.

In some ways, this situation was the ultimate test for both the staff and I, but despite doing everything in our power that evening to overcome what were unexpected problems, we all returned home that night feeling very depressed and despondent.

There was no doubting that our reputation had taken a bitter setback following this disastrous night, with the local press having a veritable field day at our expense, its press headlines declaring; 'Riot at Town Youth House!' followed by some rather over-exaggerated sensational reporting of the event.

The centre underwent a relatively quiet and generally 'incident free' period following this tempest, and life in the Youth House started to take on a sense of normality for the next few months. It was also reassuring to hear a few days later, after the event, the vast majority of the skinhead faction voicing genuine regret over the behaviour of a small minority that night.

Despite a very heavy work schedule together with my frequent visits to Norwich, I remained in constant touch with Mum, but I was very alarmed when she suffered a minor stroke that had left her with a slight speech impediment. In the meantime, she had been able to secure a very modest two-bedroom flat in a Council-owned block, very close to Redhill Station. She seemed very content in her new surroundings and appeared to have made a reasonably good recovery, despite some minor on-going difficulty she had with her speech occasionally.

Whilst endeavouring to maintain close relationships with the local press, I had become very friendly with a young reporter, Steve Harley, at the Colchester Express, and we would go on to share many a pint together. Steve suffered from a slight limp which he explained had come about when suffering with polio during his early childhood. This handicap in no way diminished his contagious dynamism and determination, and we became very close friends. Steve often shared with me some of his musical lyrics and his compulsive passion for 'pop' music. I had no appreciation at the time that this particular Steve Harley would go on to form a rock group called 'Cockney Rebel' and in 1975 produce a top selling record called 'Make me Smile'.

Steve was clearly quite well connected in the pop world and suggested that he could get a least three top headline groups to come to Colchester and perform a free gig to help raise money for the Youth House. Following the East of Eden fiasco over a year previously, I was very apprehensive. It had been a long time since that incident although generally the skinhead element now formed the core membership of the centre and had integrated well, with two of the group now on the Members Committee. Finally, I agreed to his proposal, with him suggesting that it could possibly be an Outdoor Music Festival Event over the summer, as such an event would accommodate a larger number of young people and thus raise considerably more funds for the centre.

Steve was very confident, given his various contacts, that he would be able to persuade at least three top headline groups to participate. In the meantime, I gave a lot of thought to the actual outdoor location, feeling it needed to be somewhere accessible, yet at the same time, not close to any residential area with the anticipated numbers such an event would attract and subsequent volume level.

SKINHEADS AND 'BOVVER' BOOTS!

On the centre's Management Committee was a serving officer in the Army, the Adjutant at Colchester's Garrison, Major Bushell. When I shared with him the idea about an Outdoor Music Festival, he was most enthusiastic and immediately suggested the Garrison as a potential location. He pointed out that the entrance to the Garrison would be an ideal place to collect entrance fees with nearby a substantial field, where it would be relatively easy to set up a stage and provide generator power for both lighting and the music groups' equipment. As an event like this would potentially attract large numbers, he further suggested recruiting at least 20 or 30 Garrison soldiers to help with the supervision.

The Major was an exceptionally supportive individual, and I arranged a site visit along with Steve to reconnoitre the suggested area and we agreed that the proposed location was ideal for our needs. Steve also confirmed a date in August when he had managed to get three well known groups to come to perform for us.

The next few months followed with a good deal of frenetic activity for our first ever Outdoor Music Festival, accompanied by widespread and extensive publicity. Before the event had taken place, we had already sold more than 300 tickets in advance at £5 a head and anticipated that upwards of at least a thousand young people could potentially attend. The concert was scheduled to kick off at 8:00pm with the three musical groups each doing a set of four numbers, concluding around 11.00/11:30 pm.

Only one lingering concern was the unpredictable weather, despite being held in August, being as there was no cover close to the field where the Festival was to be staged. As it transpired, it was to be a gloriously hot sunny day that would continue through to the evening and we all saw this as a good omen.

By 8.00 pm the event had already attracted well over 700 paying young guests with yet more young people arriving. This was very comforting for Steve and the many staff who had kindly volunteered to help supervise on that evening (together with the Major's 20 or so soldiers). We were all simply 'over the moon' about how the evening was progressing and by 9:30pm the first group had completed their musical set with an exhilarating atmosphere beginning to build.

Suddenly, a general commotion could be heard at the entrance area and a few staff members and myself headed in that direction. By that time a group of about 15 skinheads, clearly very intoxicated, had barged their way past the entrance staff shouting obscenities as they ran towards the field and open-air concert. Within minutes this disruptive group had cut a swathe through the gathered audience head-butting as many people as they could. It was another case of *'déjà vu'!!*

The evening quickly descended into a total fiasco with the musical groups having wisely abandoned the stage and hordes of young people forming a mass exodus flocking to get out. Meanwhile some of the Major's soldiers had confronted a few of the group who had caused the kerfuffle and were embroiled in scuffles as the situation escalated out of control. By 10:00 pm police squad cars had arrived on the site and several arrests made, bringing the evening to a premature conclusion with the staff and myself feeling we needed to be sedated!

The ensuring adverse publicity was, as we had expected. This also included a brief mention on Anglian Television the following evening. 'Youth House Outdoor Music Festival Riot' dominated the local press headlines on the Monday. What was very reassuring to me, however, was the complete and total solidarity by the centre's Management Committee, with Major Bushell especially supportive.

Due principally to the dedication of the excellent staff team, life at the centre gradually took on an atmosphere of stability with much emphasis on creating a sense of belonging. Many of the original skinhead group now constituted the main core of the membership. Whilst Steve and I continued to meet a few times following that fateful evening, predictably our career paths took us in diametrically different directions. He subsequently went on to achieve world-wide fame and fortune as the lead singer of his 'Cockney Rebel' group, whereas I remained a mere youth worker in Essex.

A few months later, however, a very reassuring incident took place one evening in the coffee bar that went some way to vindicate our overall philosophy and commitment and a tangible example of it. A new young member was already stretched out with his boots on one of the coffee tables and before I had time to react, one of the skinhead youngsters promptly walked over to the young man and said quite assertively: "Oi Mate! You don't put your boots on our coffee tables in our club, so get 'em off the table, ok!" It was one of those very rare 'Eureka' moments!

An outstanding maintenance and cleaning staff also ensured that the Youth House always looked immaculate and pristine, thus upholding my own strong views about maintaining high standards. Early on in my career, I had read a very compelling article in 'The Times Educational Supplement' with the heading: 'Low standards only serve to create low expectations'. This went on to shape, in a very pivotal way, my own professional youth work beliefs and philosophy. I also felt very passionately that every human being possessed an innate ability, irrespective of background or circumstances, and that the goal of education was to extract and nourish this.

Some of the young skinhead fraternity often found themselves in trouble with the law and I was often called to the County Crown Court in the County Town, Chelmsford, to give character references. Invariably, despite my best efforts, most of them as repeat offenders, ended up with custodial sentences.

By our second year, the centre was a hive of activity with a substantial membership and an active Youth Members Committee who determined and exercised a code of discipline within the centre, with two members on the main Management Committee. We were also one of the first youth centres in the country to run an alcoholic bar for the over-18s, in collaboration with a local jazz club, boosting our membership by a further thousand members. Other key developments included a daily lunch club for young people as well as people in the community, hiring the facilities during the daytime to local Schools, Colleges and Adult Education Classes and providing much needed revenue for the Youth House, and bringing with it enhanced kudos, following the earlier challenges.

On a personal level, I was enjoying something of a local status within the community, receiving regular invitations to the Mayor's Annual Ball and other prestigious events. And being frequently invited to give talks to local Rotary, Round Table and Women's Institutes, in addition to featuring in numerous articles in the local press.

The Youth House's reputation was also now being felt in the county, with regular visits by trainees from the county's Youth Training Scheme. However, this highly successful period of growth would not have been possible without an enormous team effort and the support of the Members and Management Committees.

Despite this powerhouse of activity, I still managed some personal leisure time with several Saturday nights' entertainment in the local Andromeda Club, as well as visiting Mum as often as I could. It was also a significant and important time for the country, with the introduction of metric weights and measures and the first ever UK referendum on the European Common Market.

1969 was also a momentous year for humanity when Astronaut Neil Armstrong stepped onto the moon's surface with the immortal words, "That's one small step for man, one giant leap for mankind."

It was also a period characterised by a 'wind of change' blowing most definitely through the Youth Service in Essex, following the appointment of Eric Hopwood, the new County Youth Officer. A person renowned for a 'no nonsense', uncompromising reputation, who would ultimately go on to be yet another influential role model in my life.

Within a matter of months, Eric had already organised an Essex Youth Orchestra (one of many of his responsibilities) to undertake a musical tour of the USA, the Orchestra enjoying a highly regarded reputation, not just in the county and country, but also overseas. With more than 100 Orchestra members, assistants and instruments, Eric had chartered a Jet to transport the group to the USA. As there were to be an additional 30 or so seats available, he approached me with a view to recruiting a further group of young people to accompany the Orchestra, but undertaking a separate tour staying with hosts' families both in the USA and Canada. This was a unique opportunity which I accepted, and within a few months I had escorted this group on a successful and memorable tour of the States and Canada.

A few months later Eric approached me again, asking if I would take on the challenge of a Statutory Youth Centre based in Tilbury, where a new building was already under construction, given the considerable experience I had gained with Colchester Youth House. The current youth centre was operating temporarily in a rather run-down former Village Hall. He concluded by making me an informal offer, that when he was in a position to reorganise his Officer team, he would ensure I was short-listed for one of the posts. Eventually, Eric would be true to his words, but it would be a further two years before this became a reality.

As it had now been over four years since I had been first appointed, it seemed like an appropriate time to seek new challenges. I had no illusions whatsoever that Tilbury would certainly be a far cry from the delights of semi-rural Colchester, but I still nonetheless accepted Eric's offer.

When news broke of my pending departure, it was met with considerable surprise and disappointment. My loyal and exceedingly hard-working secretary, Freda Clark, who had been with me throughout my time at the centre, together with Eileen Blaxill, were particularly upset by my decision.

Of all the people I had met and had the pleasure of working with over my exciting, yet challenging years in Colchester, one person stood out. Eileen Blaxill. Like so many contemporaries from similar well-heeled circumstances, she could so easily have filled her time differently, but Eileen chose to dedicate and devote herself tirelessly to raising thousands of pounds for a cause that she felt passionately about – the welfare and genuine care of young people, especially those whom she felt came from a disadvantaged or deprived background. She was, without doubt in my mind, a person who possessed immense human kindness and qualities, and someone whom I greatly admired for her determination, strong willpower and personal courage, and her vision to turn Colchester Youth House from a dream to a reality.

I continued to keep in touch with Eileen and managed to see her just a few weeks before her sad death, spending her remaining years in a private nursing home near Colchester. Although I found her frail and a little hard of hearing, she remained to the end a formidable and exceptional human being and it was my great privilege, not only to be touched by her humanity, but more importantly to call her my friend.

Towards the end of serving out my notice, a most memorable farewell party was organised and held, rather appropriately, in the local Andromeda Night Club.

A few months following my departure, I was told of the appointment of my replacement, Nigel Rogers. He would go on to be one of my closest friends and I would serve as his best man at his wedding to his future wife, Edwina, a few years later.

On the horizon, Tilbury beckoned, and with it another unpredictable and challenging chapter in my life.

DEAD END TOWN

Before leaving Colchester, I had already received confirmation from the local Thurrock Council in Grays that I had been allocated a one-bedroom flat in a Council House block just a mile outside Tilbury. Six months before my departure from Colchester, I had also traded in my Mini car due to its increasing unreliability, and as my monthly salary had increased quite substantially, I took the decision to put down a deposit on a new Mini, a light mustard colour. For me, however, this move represented in so many ways, a completely fresh start – new car, accommodation, location and youth centre.

My earlier perceptions of Tilbury were, as I had fully anticipated, a grim reality. It was a harsh and depressing area blighted by pockets of deprivation and poverty and dominated by a maze of row after row of tasteless council house tower blocks; it was not difficult to understand its reputation at that time as resembling a 'Dead End' town appearance. Most of the male population were employed at the nearby Docks, a workplace with a predominately 'macho' environment. Many of the young people who would become the core membership of the centre, came from these large dock workers' extended families where physical violence and domestic abuse were common occurrences and accepted to some extent as being part of everyday life and local culture.

As I drove down to the location of the existing centre, I passed the proposed new project, the building foundation work already underway. Close-by was the Old Village Hall building with its pitched roof, peeling paint on its wooden exterior door and boarded-up windows, reflecting a generally bleak image, in keeping with much of the rest of the area, leaving me with an overwhelming feeling of being 'out of my comfort zone'. This temporary youth centre being my workplace for the foreseeable future and certainly a total contrast compared to the Youth House.

As I entered through the very heavy entrance double doors, passing through a short dark passageway to the main hall inside, I was warmly greeted by two people who would become my colleagues and friends over the coming year. Pat introduced herself as the Centre's part-time Secretary – an attractive, relatively short woman in her mid-thirties with strong physique, blond hair and a voice that resembled Barbara Windsor. I was immediately struck by her wonderfully vivacious, bubbly personality and warmth.

Pat promptly introduced me to Billy, the part-time cleaner-cum-maintenance person. A fairly tall, grey-haired man in his late sixties but from initial impressions, someone who had a most definite 'spring in his step'. Both Pat and Billy lived and had spent all their lives in Tilbury and their local knowledge would go on to become invaluable to me.

Despite the warmth of their welcome, they openly expressed surprise that I had taken on what they felt was a challenging role, defining many of the local youngsters as 'hard as nails'. Although not particularly reassuring initial observations, I was nevertheless hopeful that my earlier experience in Colchester would serve me well.

The Old Village Hall had a very substantial assembly area with a small office and store at the entrance hall end, with toilets and small coffee bar-cum-social area at the rear end. It was scrumptiously clean, no doubt due to Billy's fine efforts, but the building looked like it was on its last legs. The interior was dark and dim with an exceptionally huge open ceiling and exposed wooden beams.

That first night I was greeted by a small handful of club members who seemed somewhat bemused by my appearance as the 'new boss'. Membership was at an all-time low and given the facilities on offer that came as no surprise to me, and the only quite elderly male member of the part time staff team had already decided to quit a week later.

I set myself, therefore, a number of key objectives. Recruitment of enthusiastic staff members who had both the personality and ability to work with challenging youngsters; transform the somewhat dilapidated old village hall into something more appealing and welcoming, but most importantly, launch a programme of activities and events that would bring about a substantial growth in club membership from what was clearly a potentially strong catchment area.

I also took the opportunity to visit the local Area Youth Officer in Grays whose demeanour seemed to reflect the area's name and nature. A very elderly, grey haired, rather tired looking individual giving the distinct impression of someone just 'serving out his time'. Whilst I spoke enthusiastically about my various plans for the centre, this did not elicit any kind of positive response from him, and I could recognise immediately why Eric Hopwood wanted to re-organise his Youth Officer structure as soon as the opportunity presented itself.

Very soon I had recruited four relatively young staff (two females, two males) who quickly, due to their professional skill and understanding, forged meaningful relationship with the few members we had. My second 'mission' was also well underway. For several weeks the staff, together with the full participation of the few members, transformed the otherwise drab hall into something more aesthetically pleasing – even Pat and Billy got caught up in the enthusiasm and were often present to lend a willing hand.

With the support of the Area Building Surveyor, who was impressed by our interior building efforts and knowing that we would only occupy the building for another nine months before the completion of the new building, still agreed to a minor works programme that would considerably augment much of the self-help work we had already undertaken.

Part of my initial strategy included a visit to the nearby Secondary School to promote the centre and following my earlier instincts, we launched a weekly Friday disco evening that over the next few months attracted in excess of 150 young people. All these changes fuelled a surge in membership with the staff team going to great lengths to enhance a sense of belonging, recognising in many of the members quite low feelings of self-esteem with several from dysfunctional family backgrounds. As a hallmark of my youth work ethics, the empowerment of young people was always at the forefront of my thinking, and a members committee was quickly formed with decision-making powers.

There were, however, setbacks to these initial successes. Similarly to my early Youth House days, a small, but influential group of very deviant young people were extremely disruptive, choosing to undermine our efforts at change. These outright challenges to the staff and me took on a familiar pattern and night after night this minority were abusive to the staff and equally intimidating to the other centre members. All attempts at that stage to win them over were met with hostility and aggression. This led one night to me discovering, after the centre's closure, that the air in all my car tyres had been deflated, but I took comfort in the fact that no permanent damage had taken place.

Gradually, over time, thanks in large measure to the caring staff team who collectively overcame what seemed like insurmountable challenges, this minority finally came to terms with the change in ethos within the centre, recognising the fundamental but positive changes that had taken place and finally fully integrating into the mainstream membership.

Billy always worked very conscientiously to ensure that any minor damage in the centre was always quickly addressed, knowing that it was fundamental to my thinking that the premises always needed to reflect a sense of care, no matter how ancient it was.

Radio One was a very popular programme with young listeners at that time, especially the weekly outside broadcast that went out live from various locations around the country, attracting huge audience numbers. Somewhat optimistically, I sent a letter to the producers of the programme asking if they would consider a future live broadcast from the existing youth centre, giving details about the new project, stressing how I felt this would be an enormous morale boost for the membership and relatively depressed area.

Somehow my letter found the right person as two months later the Radio One Roadshow was being broadcast from the centre with the charismatic Alan 'Fluff' Freeman at the turntable. An hour before the programme went 'live', over 500 young people packed the old Village Hall. The broadcast was a phenomenal success that consequently did so much to raise the profile of both the centre and area.

Following this success, the membership grew substantially but it was a constant concern of the staff and myself when, at times, a member appeared looking as if they had been a victim of domestic abuse, but whenever approached, the response was invariably the same: "It's nothing, mate, just a little knock I got at football". Such worrying problems seemed to be kept fully and inextricably below the radar.

With our reputation gaining prominence in the town, whenever I happened to mention in passing to a member that it would be really helpful to get some kind of equipment, it was virtually guaranteed, 'no questions asked', a few days later that very item would be waiting outside the centre. Tilbury was a Docks town and anything 'pre-containerisation' days that generally 'fell off the back of a lorry' was very much part of everyday life!

In our quest to broaden the members' interests we were willing to risk sometimes new and innovative activities. A visit to the Royal Ballet in London to see a performance of 'Swan Lake' with ten young people – six young women and four young men – was no exception.

On arrival, the grandeur and elegance of the foyer of the Royal Opera House was enough to take the young people's breath away, but once the performance was underway, it was clear the group were totally mesmerised by what they were witnessing. After the performance all confessed to never having had such an experience before and how much they had enjoyed watching ballet dancers live on a stage. There was however a 'Molotov' cocktail moment when one of boys made a somewhat jaw dropping observation: "Blimey, Bill, those male dancers had some 'big nuts'!" I was never to find out if there may have been a potential 'Billy Elliot' in those ranks, but to me I always felt youth work should be about exploration and discovery, if only to find that some male Ballet dancers allegedly "have big nuts!".

With the new building weeks away from completion, I was becoming increasingly worried about Mum's general state of health. Thankfully, Pam, my twin sister, lived close at hand in nearby Horley, but despite this I still started applying for a full-time post within the area so I could be closer to her. A month later, I had been successful in securing a full-time post in a large Youth, Community and Adult Education Centre in Burgess Hill, just a short distance from Mum in Redhill and about ten miles from the beautiful seaside town of Brighton.

Following my appointment, I went to see Eric Hopwood, and whilst he was disappointed that I felt unable to stay to see through the transitional period to the opening of the new centre, he fully appreciated my motives. He reiterated, once again, that he was expecting to re-organise his Officer Team within the next year and that I would definitely be short-listed, if I chose to apply.

Two weeks prior to my departure from Tilbury, I went to visit my mum for the weekend in Reigate. She had been suffering severe abdominal pains and Pam was in the flat when I arrived and about to leave to collect Gary from his 'Special Education Unit'. She expressed very serious concerns for Mum's condition feeling she had generally deteriorated over the past 24 hours and had already called the doctor.

Within the hour, Mum's doctor had arrived and following examination arranged for her to be taken immediately by ambulance to the local East Surrey Hospital near Redhill. About ten minutes later, I accompanied Mum in the ambulance to the hospital where, after further examination, she was transferred to an isolation ward within the hospital.

I informed the nursing staff on the ward that I was one of her next of kin and gave them my address and line number in Tilbury. Upon returning to Mum's flat, I spent a very restless and generally sleepless night with thoughts of Mum uppermost in my mind. With a very early start the following day, I immediately telephoned the hospital. Although it seemed like an eternity before eventually being put through to the appropriate Ward Sister, I identified myself and immediately her voice became quite agitated and she said: "Mr Palmer, I am sorry, but your mother's condition is giving us cause for concern, so please can you come as soon as possible". With such ominous news I left very soon after but rang both my sisters to inform them of the situation.

When I arrived at the room where I had last seen Mum, the bed had been completely stripped and a cleaning lady was mopping the area. Suddenly, the Ward Sister came rushing in looking very anxious and directed me to a small ante-room. She sat me down and in a very consoling way uttered words that would resonate with me for the rest of my life. "I am dreadfully sorry to tell you, Mr Palmer, but your mother suffered a massive cerebral haemorrhage in the early hours of this morning and passed away. I can assure you that she suffered no pain and died peacefully. We had tried unsuccessfully to contact you at your Tilbury address but despite repeated efforts we were unable to get a response. I am so very sorry to have to break this very sad news to you. Please accept my sincerest condolences."

I was totally numb and consumed with suppressed emotions, especially haunted by the cruel irony that unbeknown I was within the immediate vicinity the night before. I asked to see my mum and the Ward Sister kindly directed me to the Chapel of Rest where Mum lay before being transferred to the Hospital morgue for a post-mortem examination.

Like Dad, Mum was still in her early fifties. She had been a devoted and dedicated mother and wife who supported Dad throughout his life in spite of his challenging and difficult health battles. Mum had been an extraordinarily wonderful human being who had always encouraged and supported me, as well as my two sisters. Losing one parent was in itself a harrowing experience, but to lose both prematurely within such a short period, was both brutal and devasting.

In the Chapel of Rest, Mum lay covered under a white sheet looking remarkably serene and tranquil, and where for the last time I bent over and kissed her cheek as the tears trickled down my face.

Pam and Barbara and family arrived at the Hospital shortly afterwards and were visibly shaken by the news of Mum's unexpected death. Pam was particularly distressed as she had become much closer to Mum over the time she had settled in Redhill, with her being nearby.

I arranged to stay on for a few more days to make all the appropriate funeral arrangements and to sell what little furniture and possessions Mum had, together with a small pension lump sum that just covered the expenses. I remember thinking to myself what a very modest sum it was, given a lifetime of devotion and hard work.

Mum was cremated a week later in the Surrey & Sussex Crematorium where Dad had been cremated just a few years earlier. A befitting end, as well as appropriate resting place, where once again, they could be re-united.

Shortly afterwards, Mum's local council informed me that I could continue with the tenancy of the flat as she had thoughtfully included me as part of the household, thus giving me automatic rights. I declined the offer as I was planning to rent an apartment close to Brighton, a few miles from my new location. With council dwellers given the right to purchase council properties as homeowners a few years later, it would be one of those impulsive decisions I would come to regret.

I bid farewell to all my colleagues and friends back in Tilbury who had been so supportive to me, especially Pat and Billy. Whilst I could have argued a case for staying after Mum's sudden death and knowing Eric Hopwood would have been content for me to continue at Tilbury, I nevertheless felt professionally honour-bound to take up the new appointment in Burgess Hill.

The large Youth, Community and Adult Education Centre was already very well established in the area with an exceptionally experienced staff team. With three floors, this late Victorian styled building had undergone some modernisation a few years earlier and the many large rooms enabled it to provide a host of both day and evening Youth, Community and Adult Education activities.

Knowing from the outset that my time at the Centre was likely to be limited, I still committed myself knowing also how the Community and Adult Education aspects of the Centre would become areas of learning and professional development that would bring benefits later in my career.

An integral part of my responsibilities was hosting a weekly lunch-time club for local retirees, which I enjoyed enormously, especially hearing about their very interesting and often intriguing life stories. It also gave me an opportunity to observe at close hand the various mannerisms and idiosyncratic behaviour of many of these elderly folks. A few years later, after returning and settling in Essex and becoming an active member of a local drama group, I would be given credit for my portrayal of an elderly butler in William Douglas-Home's play 'Lloyd George Knew My Father', and I put this performance down entirely to the keen observations made during my Burgess Hill days.

Towards the end of my first year, Eric Hopwood would, as he had promised, invite me to an interview in Chelmsford where I was successfully offered the post of Youth Officer for the Braintree and Witham Area. Having by that time spent ten years as a full-time Youth Worker, I felt it was the appropriate time to move up to an Officer position, confident that I would be able to use that valuable experience in an area-wide capacity.

A month later, content that I had maintained a period of stability and continuity on my watch, I left Burgess Hill at the end of December 1974 and headed back up to the flat lands of Essex. By now I had already been in touch with Joy Donnelly in Colchester, who offered me another of her magnificent flats to rent.

"NOT A SPADE, BUT A BLOODY SHOVEL"

In so many ways, this promotion would be a 'leap of faith', as no longer would I be having direct nightly contact with young people, but working through other adults who would have that responsibility.

By the time I had started on my first day in the office in Braintree, I had already gained a new professional title: Assistant Community Education Officer. Although my duties were to remain basically the same, Eric Hopwood had now been promoted to the position of Senior Education Officer, with him having, in addition to Youth Services, responsibility for a much more diverse and expanded Further Education portfolio which included Adult Education, Community Centres and the Government's new National Initiative, 'Youth Opportunities Programme', an on-the-job training course for school leavers aged 16 and 17.

Over the few years that Eric Hopwood had worked in Essex, he had already acquired a widespread reputation as a somewhat pugnacious rottweiler who did not 'suffer fools gladly'. He was fiercely proud of his Lancastrian upbringing with a: "not a spade, but a bloody shovel" approach. A workaholic by nature, he could often be abrasive, confrontational and verbally aggressive. The wise avoided him on one of his 'off' days or risk being bombarded by one of his frequent 'pink perils'; usually quite savage notes written always on a pink note-pad. If you didn't stand your ground with Eric (although that was easier said than done), your chances of becoming quickly emasculated were greatly increased.

Eric was a man in his early fifties, short and stocky, and very much resembling at that time the Labour Party's George Brown in appearance and some might have said, persona. Eric, or "EH" as he would come to be known, was vehemently opposed to any type of youth work provision he considered to have social work overtones. Detached or outreach youth work were a complete anathema to him, and he was absolutely uncompromising in this view. Eric, however, was totally committed to mainstream youth work with the emphasis on providing good quality youth work settings and offering young people a range of activities and events, including an extensive programme of overseas youth projects.

No matter his abundant and somewhat juggernaut approach, he was, without question, a dynamic visionary who devoted himself passionately to offering young people every opportunity to participate in new experiences. He provided strong and powerful leadership and was fiercely protective of those who gained his confidence and trust. In time, I came to admire his boundless energy and vitality, but more importantly, his unmistakable commitment to the social development of young people.

Whilst his strident style and uncompromising behaviour was unpopular in some quarters (and would be regarded in the future as bordering on 'bullying'), he was a highly respected Officer by the majority of County Councillors of Essex, several who would be regular witnesses to the many phenomenal high profile and prestigious events he would organise, many of which I was professionally involved with.

In my area, I quickly established a significant rapport with a large group of part-time youth workers and one of the four full-time staff, gaining their confidence and support. However, the other three full-time workers manifestly lacked any motivation and commitment, demonstrated by their conspicuous lack of involvement in county events and renowned amongst other county colleagues as being difficult to work with.

After 18 months, whilst undergoing an existential period of severe depression, I suffered a minor break-down. This was attributable in part to the three full-time workers, exacerbated by their stubborn resistance to my numerous overtures to get them and their respective youth centres to fully engage. Their on-going obstinacy took its toll on me emotionally and I interpreted this as a professional shortcoming and weakness on my part. Mental health problems would go on to blight several periods in my life, when I would struggle with very negative thoughts and actions.

Fortunately, I had a most perceptive doctor in Colchester who recognised my symptoms and immediately signed me off work for three months, prescribing medication. It was also during this period when, once again, albeit fleetingly, I started to question my own sexuality.

Notwithstanding his often-volatile nature, Eric Hopwood was nevertheless extremely supportive and very understanding throughout this dark emotional period in my life. I was also fortunate to have the support of close friends Nigel and Edwina Rogers, my niece Beverley and her husband, Hugh.

Eric's compassion stretched to him offering me another area posting, covering Central Essex, with office accommodation situated in the County Town, Chelmsford. This relatively large area comprised principally part-time centres, many based in school campuses. However, I would very soon discover that these centres enjoyed substantial memberships and were led by a dream team of very experienced and supportive part-time staff, together with two very committed full-time youth workers, one based in a Youth & Adult Education Centre in Maldon and the other a youth centre in Galleywood, on the outskirts of Chelmsford.

Now fully rejuvenated, but smoking very heavily by now, I was greeted on my first day back at work by a very stunning, quite tall, dark haired, brown eyed elegantly dressed women (who looked in her early thirties, but was actually 39), Sally, my full-time secretary. She was married and had a 14-year-old daughter Anne, and 18-year-old son, John. However, it took several months before she was confident to reveal to me that she was experiencing martial problems (that would become irreconcilable) on account of her husband's habitual extra-marital 'affairs'. Within a year, Sally and I had started a 'clandestine' relationship but somehow, we ensured that this did not compromise our professional relationship.

The daily 50-mile drive from Colchester to my new base was now beginning to become a tiring routine and finally I secured a small, but relatively comfortable studio apartment near the office. Within two years, the combination of leading a very hectic professional but somewhat restrained social life, together with a moderately good salary, enabled me to acquire a mortgage for a small three-bedroom semi-detached house on a new housing development a few miles north of the town, a place I could at last call 'home' and fulfilling a long-held ambition.

Although working with EH was an all-encompassing experience, consuming so much of one's life, it was in so many ways both stimulating as well as unpredictable, not knowing what innovative project was up his sleeve and yet to be unleashed. Most of my evenings were occupied with visiting and supporting the part-time centres in my area, and at weekends organising the various heats for the myriad county events, competitions and activities that were now integral to a comprehensive programme.

Within two years, with local support and commercial sponsorship, I staged the first of what would go on in my professional life to be several 'Youth Spectaculars'; variety performances that showcased the very best of youth talent. This first, and subsequent shows would see a rewarding number of young people pursue professional career paths within the theatre, television and film industries.

In spite of a very hectic professional life, my own keen interest in the theatre led me to joining a very distinguished amateur dramatics group in Little Baddow near Chelmsford, who enjoyed an exceptional reputation for staging impressive productions. My first involvement was the pantomime 'Aladdin' when director Mo Bright (a former professional dancer), cast me into several minor roles, including being a 'rock' on stage. My association with the group would go on to last several years with me occasionally taking the lead in a few evergreen productions of Alan Ayckbourn's comedy plays.

One person I became very close to through the club was an openly 'gay' man, John Richardson ('JR' to his many friends), a most accomplished actor who remained a friend for many years long after I had left Essex. It was when, still in his early sixties, that John suffered a massive heart attack from which he would not recover. John's 'am-dram' legacy, however, would be his performance and portrayal as the elder brother in the very dramatic play by American playwright, Arthur Miller, 'All My Sons'. That incredibly emotional performance justifiably earned him wide-spread plaudits as well as being the recipient of a prestigious best amateur actor award in the region.

As a strong advocate of young people's empowerment, I soon formed an Area Youth Council who in close liaison with me, worked on various local youth issues. The Chairman of this group was a young man of 18 years, Darryl Hooker, an exceptionally bright individual who in some ways became something of a prodigy. His talents were very quickly recognised by EH and once established, he would also be elected to the Chair of the first-ever county-wide Youth Council. Darryl and I would go on to be life-long friends, with my wife Sally and I attending his marriage to a beautiful young woman, Helen. With the birth of their two sons, Danny and Perry, they eventually settled in a town not dissimilar to the popular sixties television series, 'Peyton Place', in the suburbs of New York, a place I would visit on two occasions and where Darryl pursued a highly successful career in the financial world. However, their marriage broke down a few years later, leading to divorce, when the boys were in their late teens. Darryl would go on to marry an attractive American woman, Jackie, and they had one son Harrison, and 15 years later settled back in the UK and set up home near Chelmsford in Essex.

Following the highly successful Youth Orchestra trip to the USA, EH went on to pioneer and expand fully an imaginative programme of overseas projects. I was personally involved in several with visits to Rome, Genoa and the spectacular island of Sardinia, where three annual youth projects were held, including groups from Italy and Germany. I also led a group on a somewhat formidable skiing trip to the communist capital of Romania, at that time under the notoriously oppressive dictatorship of Nicolae Ceausescu and his equally complicit wife. Whilst the accommodation and food were very basic, the ski-slopes and equipment were of a high standard, but more importantly, it gave the young people in the party an invaluable insight into a totalitarian political regime.

One significant highlight in the Essex Youth Service calendar was the annual International Youth Camp, attracting over 500 young people and leaders from most European countries, including a group from Israel. This was held in August at the county's extensive campsite at East Mersea, on the Island of

Mersea, and was a well-established event that had operated successfully for many years. I was given the responsibility of running the vast and time-consuming entertainment programme for a number of years. One notable triumph was my success in persuading, for the second time, the BBC to stage its Radio One Live Outside Broadcast at the Campsite. On this occasion it was the very outgoing personality of Ed Stewart (who was also known as "StewPot") who graced the microphone and hosted what was an outstanding success.

Not all the events I was involved with gained such accolades. After staging the successful Youth Spectaculars in my area, EH pressured me into organising and compering the annual County Talent Contest, one of the flagship events. One unforgettable and infamous year was when it was staged at the local theatre in Billericay, with a capacity audience. One of the finalists, following area heats, was a musical pop group of young lads. Unbeknown to Robin Rhodes, a friend I had enlisted as stage manager, having been previously involved with the Youth Spectacular shows, this young group of 'wannabees' were the worse for wear having indulged in a heavy drinking session in the 'green room'. Back on stage, Robin had already sussed out the situation and the likely repercussions but by that time unable to convey his concerns to me, having already introduced the group as the main stage curtains were parting. For a perilous few minutes, the young lads hammered away at their guitars and drum set, complete with obscenities like some 'copycat' version of the 'Sex Pistols'. Before completing their final number, the curtains were quickly dropped and Robin and his crew cleared the equipment and lads off the stage in preparation for the next act, whilst I attempted, somewhat nonchalantly and with a degree of composure, to play down the incident to a rather bewildered, and by now, confused audience.

The panel of judges on that night included Mo Bright, Darryl Hooker and alas, EH, who was incandescent with anger following the show. The rest of the programme went without further hitches and the now sobered up lads full of apologies. Many in the audience, however, were convinced it was just a feature of the lads' act!

By now Sally's marriage had ended in divorce, and she and Anne, now 19, came to live with me. When news of this reached EH, he felt it important that Sally continue to work within the Service, but no longer with me, which I fully understood and felt eminently sensible. Sally was therefore transferred to a good training post within the Youth Opportunities Programme. I had a new, quite young Secretary, Janet, to replace Sally, who not only was highly efficient but fitted in very well after her departure.

Since becoming a Youth Officer, I had adopted an 'open door' policy and 'management by walkabout' *modus operandi* style of working, which I would maintain throughout my professional youth work career. One day, Janet informed me that there was a woman outside wanting to see me by the name of Krysia Dodson, enquiring about the possibility of part-time paid youth work and I invited her in. Before me stood a woman I speculated to be in her late thirties, with long flowing hair, dressed in a 'hippy' style long outfit complete with red laced-up boots and reminiscent of the 'flower power' period.

After a brief conversation, I realised I had before me an exceptionally caring and intelligent woman who I immediately felt would make a fantastic addition to our part-time team and I offered her a post in one of the centres, which she accepted. Within a few months, Krysia's working style, a combination of care and empathy, was having a very major influence upon other workers, as well as the young people. When a vacancy for a part-time Leader in Charge occurred in a centre on the perimeter of Chelmsford, an area renowned for predominately anti-social youth behaviour, Krysia's name immediately sprung to mind, and I subsequently offered her the position, which she accepted.

I accompanied Krysia on the first night of her visit to the Centre so she could be introduced to the other part-time members of staff. Amongst them was a particularly strong-minded male member, but quite experienced. When I introduced Krysia as their new Leader in Charge, his reaction was unambiguous: "Sorry, Bill, I've never had a female 'boss' before and I don't intend to start now." To me, equality of opportunity was ingrained within my philosophy and outlook, and therefore Krysia's gender was totally irrelevant, and she had been appointed the next Leader. The man in question left the centre and Krysia went on to be one of the most outstanding workers in the area – a real gold dust as far as I was concerned.

There was also to be another very gifted person who walked into my office one day that would have a profound impact upon my life, as well as many other people touched by her humanity. Her name was Liz Nunn. A relatively short person, fairly large in physique, with greying hair and piercing blue eyes, and as I was to discover later, in her early seventies. Whatever she may have lacked in size and stature, was more than compensated by her immense energy, vitality and dedication.

Liz shared with me her India experiences, telling me how she had visited the country many times over the past two years and had become increasingly distressed at some of the poverty she had witnessed. She had become especially concerned about the plight of many thousands of homeless and parentless children, some as young as six or seven, who spent much of their lives scavenging at many of the city's waste disposal dumps to eke out what was for most a desperate existence, and sleeping in the open on the streets every night and subject to all kinds of abuse. These young people were often referred to as 'Rag Pickers'.

Liz went on to tell me that she had, as a direct result of her experiences, established a UK charity that she had titled: 'Friends of the Lotus Children' and had also persuaded the Liberal Democrats' Leader and Member of Parliament, Paddy Ashdown, to be one of its founding Presidents, with a purpose to set up shelters for these young kids. She had given the Charity its title because she had known that the lotus flower was regarded as a magical flower rooted in mud but somehow found a way to bloom and grow. She thought this perfectly reflected the lives of so many of these young 'Rag Pickers'.

She was living in Milton Keynes at the time, but one of her relatives lived in Chelmsford and had spoken about my work in the area and she had come to see me in the hope that

I might be able to help raise funds locally for her Charity and get young people involved. Her obvious commitment and conviction impressed me enormously but nevertheless I asked her to leave the proposition with me and promised to get back to her.

A few days later, I spoke to EH and shared with him the long conversation I had had with Liz and how very impressed I was by what she was attempting to achieve, given her age and somewhat frail disposition. I suggested to him that we could circulate publicity about the Charity within the County Youth Service and Schools and look to recruit 15 young people to accompany Liz on a future tour of India so that they could witness first-hand the problems that existed, and on return these young people would then have to commit themselves over the following year to raising a minimum of £1,000 each. Also, the group collectively, would determine which area they considered could benefit most by the establishment of a shelter for these 'Rag Pickers'. The genesis for this idea being my own VSO life-changing experience. His response was a little unexpected: "Ok, lad, get on with it, and if it goes ahead, you can also accompany the group".

Over the next six months, I had been able to secure a grant from the Commonwealth Youth Exchange to cover all the air fares and internal travel, with Liz arranging host family accommodation in India. Fifteen young people, all aged 17 (nine young women and six young men) had been selected from a significant number of applicants. A residential weekend was held so the young people could become more knowledgeable about the history, culture and development of India, with Liz sharing her experiences with them. Our discussions stressing that not only would they be visiting one of the oldest civilisations in the world with the largest democracy, but a country from whom they could also learn a great deal and that this was not to be regarded as some kind of 'colonial-minded' project, but a journey of discovery and learning.

Liz, along with the Charity's Treasurer, a charming man called Peter, a fellow excellent female officer colleague Marilyn Lewis, 15 very excitable young people and me, took a flight in the early summer to Mumbai. After an intensive, but memorable three weeks, travelling by train from Mumbai to the far south city of Cochin, the young people had evaluated many prospective shelter sites en route. It was an amazing experience for everyone in the party to get up close to the immense problems that Liz had highlighted, but also just as importantly, to embrace a fantastic culture and meet many wonderful Indian people along the way.

One final, and lasting memory, as the group boarded a minibus for the return journey from the airport, was a young Indian boy. No more than seven or eight years of age, he was seated on a small, flat wooden trolley with wheels, his legs amputated from the knees down but waving, with a big unforgettable smile, yet never once attempting to beg. The young people subsequently collected all their loose remaining rupees and handed it to him. It was not a particularly significant amount of money, but the boy was clearly overjoyed. As the minibus pulled away, he did his best to keep up, waving and smiling and shouting "Shukriya, Shukriya" ('Thank you' in Hindi) until the bus was out of sight.

A year later, at a ceremony in County Hall, a cheque for over £25,000 was handed over to Liz and the Charity to establish three Shelters in Mumbai, Bangalore and Cochin, entirely raised by the young people. I remained in touch with Liz and the Charity for many years afterwards and was honoured to become its National Vice-Chairman for several years. Liz Nunn went on to receive an OBE for her services to young people, something that delighted everyone touched by her humanity and selflessness; an award in recognition of her dedication and devotion to the 'Rag Pickers' of Indian. I heard a few years later that she had returned her medal in protest at the second Gulf War and invasion of Iraq. This act confirming everything I already knew about this quite extraordinary woman.

Liz passed away in her mid-eighties and to the very end of her life was raising awareness and funds to draw attention to the plight of her beloved 'Rag Pickers'. But she had already left behind a remarkable legacy that few people could ever have expected to achieve in their lifetime and her remarkable spirit would live on.

One innovative project that gave me a great deal of professional satisfaction before I left Essex, was the acquisition of a second-hand double-decker bus. With the help of volunteers, complete with a range of appropriate skills, the bus was converted into a mobile youth project, complete with coffee bar and toilet. Its principal aim was to serve the rural hinterland of Central Essex, for which there was no existing youth service provision.

Eric Hopwood would also go on to establish another groundbreaking project with the formation of the Essex Dance Theatre, under its highly distinguished Director, Debbie Holme. This was created in recognition of how dance could be employed as a successful catalyst in developing young people's personal and social development, at the same time channelling their energies and talent. It subsequently became an acknowledged integral part of the Community Education Service in Essex.

Eric was also passionately committed to the Duke of Edinburgh's Award Scheme that had been created by Prince Phillip in 1956 to promote and develop learning and life skills amongst young people. EH would eventually become a National Trustee of the Scheme and in recognition of his work with young people, both at home and overseas, was awarded a well-earned OBE honour before his retirement.

In the autumn of 1986 wedding bells were ringing in the air when Sally and I finally got married at a registry office wedding ceremony in Chelmsford, with Hugh serving as my best man. It was one of the happiest days of my life and I loved Sally very deeply. Many people felt we were a very compatible couple, given our respective personalities complementing each other; Sally always thinking things through very carefully, whereas I was, more often than not, compelled to make rash and often impulsive decisions. It was a time when I genuinely felt that any lurking 'gay' feelings were, once and for all, laid to rest.

After nearly 14 years as an Area Youth Officer, I felt the time was right to contemplate a career move and shortly after our marriage in the November, I applied and had been invited to interview, over a two-day period, in the Dorset County town of Dorchester for the post of Assistant County Youth Officer, which would represent a significant promotion for me.

The incumbent County Youth Officer, Ted Watkins, a man in his late fifties, quite tall, stocky and grey haired, had an exceptionally quiet personality and disposition, and my impression of a somewhat avuncular character. On the day of the interviews, other candidates and I shared our collective surprise, given that the person appointed would become Ted's right-hand, that he appeared to take a limited involvement in the first day's interview process with this being driven by the Principal Education Officer, John Cooper.

Of the original eight candidates, three, including myself, were short-listed the next day, following a tour of local youth centres the evening before. The interview panel included the Deputy County Education Officer, Richard Ely, the Chair of the Education Committee, Mrs Pamela Seaton, and Ted Watkins. At the conclusion of the second day, I was offered the post, which I accepted. In so many ways this was another auspicious and defining moment in my life. I was quite euphoric following my success as was Sally and the many colleagues who were delighted by news of my future posting. Even EH seemed to take some disguised pleasure when hearing the news.

Sally and I agreed that she should remain behind in Essex for the first few months of my appointment so she could continue with her relatively new position as Secretary to the Mayor of Southend-on-Sea, a post she was finding very fulfilling.

Once again, after yet another memorable farewell party, I started preparing for my imminent departure to Thomas Hardy's 'Far from the Madding Crowd' County, to start my new position from the beginning of 1987.

Indian rag picker

NEW BROOM THAT SWEEPS CLEAN

Prior to commencing my appointment, I had been able to secure a small furnished rental house just a few miles out of Dorchester, with Sally remaining behind as we had agreed. As a final settlement to her divorce, she had retained the matrimonial home from her previous marriage where she would live during this interim period.

The headquarters of the service was located in County Hall, Dorchester, and my arrival coincided with a very much needed and overdue internal modernisation programme. Located in the cavern-like basement area, the corridors leading to the four offices accommodating the seven HQ staff, were dark, ill-lit, rather grim and virtually inaccessible. In many ways, as I was soon to discover, the very embodiment of the service I had recently signed up to!

It soon became distinctly clear to me that Ted, as Head of the service, felt himself under immense pressure and that was outwardly demonstrated by his hesitant manner and general temperament. Yet, with over 60 full-time and 400 part-time youth posts and 13 field officers, Dorset was considered one of the best resourced youth services in the country with an annual budget in excess of three million pounds. Despite large conurbations in Bournemouth and Poole, Dorset's financial support far exceeded those counties with larger populations and geographical size. Whilst it had been a distant dream for most other authorities to unveil a new youth centre building, Dorset had retained a very active capital building programme with virtually a new youth centre built every four years.

My introduction to the 13 Officers took place at a meeting during my first week and only served to heighten my initial apprehensions and concerns. The group was totally male dominated with at least 80% in their late fifties/early sixties. However, the minority of younger officers were clearly looking for change, having become disillusioned and frustrated by Ted's lack of positive leadership and general style of taking a back seat and uncommitted attitude to any form of po-active action. This polarised situation strengthened my belief that Ted was presiding over a fractured and fractious group. It was also clearly evident that his health was declining, as he always appeared tired and listless, giving the distinct impression of being slightly indifferent to any ideas that many felt were some of the immediate challenges facing the service.

In one conversation, after the meeting, I was somewhat dismayed when two of the youth officer group declared themselves as 'Freemasons' and three others as 'Born again Christians', a consortium of 'funny hand shakers' and 'spiritual re-birthers' which I found disconcerting as if somehow this was a pronouncement of virtue.

Over the next few weeks, I toured all the youth centres in the county and what I was to find only reinforced my growing pessimism about the vast majority of full-time youth centres. I was witnessing, not only very low levels of membership attendances, but virtually no evidence of any form of social education, a commitment to youth empowerment, equal opportunities and the promotion of life and social skills. What was on display, however, was the existence of low levels of recreational activity and what little positive evidence I did see was principally male dominated programmes, with the role of young women generally subjugated.

I was totally shocked by what I was unearthing, together with a general lack of accountability and transparency by some workers and officers, the majority on comparable salaries to the teaching profession. Many of these centres would not have met the criteria for the establishment of a full-time post in Essex, in particular in my last area posting, where part-time centres had considerably larger memberships and demonstrably good youth work practices. It was hardly surprising that by my third month in post, I was already acquiring a reputation as a person intent on becoming the proverbial 'new broom that sweeps clean'; someone, potentially, to disrupt the congenial 'status quo' and for a few I came close to earning the epithet 'Tiller the Hun'.

A small, but somewhat troglodyte group had also begun to gain momentum with an uncompromising '*fait accompli*' to what they claimed as accepted 'custom and practice', which included one session a week out of ten sessions (a session defined as a morning, afternoon or evening) devoted to professional 'support'. I was not aware of any other profession that allowed this kind of employment doctrine. Given, ironically, that the birth of trade unionism was founded in the village of Tolpuddle, just a few miles from the County town, Dorchester, this practice seemed to me to be totally out of step with even the most radical employment advances.

By now I began seriously exploring with Sally over one of my weekends back in Chelmsford, about applying for other senior Youth Officer appointments that might become vacant. Moreover, I was very relieved Sally had not given up her Mayor's Secretary post to join me at that stage, as I was becoming increasing aware that I had become quite a divisive figure in the eyes of some who regarded me as a potential threat; thus I had become embroiled in unwittingly sowing seeds of opposition and dissent. On a career level, I was beginning to feel that I had landed up in some professional *'cul de sac'* and that the prospect of staying in Dorset for any length of time seemed highly improbable.

However, over the next few months, three significant and unexpected factors emerged that would ultimately secure my relatively long-term future relationship with Dorset Youth Service. Feeling what he perceived as mounting pressure, Ted had begun to exhibit yet more stress and eventually we received news that he had been signed off by his local doctor for the foreseeable future, owing to his ill health.

The Principal Education Officer and Ted's immediate Line Manager was John Cooper. An exceptionally short person, in his early sixties with grey hair and a very distinguished handlebar moustache, John had a distinctive military bearing whenever he walked anywhere, using his umbrella on most days like some Regimental Colonel reviewing a squad of soldiers, and also having a reputation for being a very accomplished amateur golfer.

John had spent most of his career before settling in Dorset, working in West Africa as an Area Education Officer and responsible for a geographical area twice the size of Dorset. He was a very well educated and extremely well-spoken man and was held in high regard by many in the Education Department. John offered me the post of Acting Youth Officer during Ted's absence, a position that I accepted in spite of my earlier misgivings, and my first positive piece of good news.

Operating within the County was also an alliance of both the Voluntary and Statutory sectors on a County-wide Youth Service Committee under the Chairmanship of Reverend Ian Johnson, Church Deacon for a Parish in Wimborne Minster. Given the substantial allocated annual youth service budget, concerns were growing about what many felt was an increasingly moribund service in danger of inertia, in many ways supporting the veracity of my own findings. It was therefore proposed and agreed, that a county-wide review be undertaken, and Ian and I were tasked with overseeing a working party and subsequently to produce a report of our findings.

Questionnaires were circulated to all youth centres in the county, both voluntary and statutory, County Councillors and other major services – Police, Probation, Social Services, Health Services, Charities etc – to ascertain views on the current level of youth service provision. Interpreting the feedback from questionnaires together with several area discussion groups, Ian and I collaborated very closely over the next month to produce a report we titled: 'Time for Youth', much of the content of the report written up by Ian.

Although I had deliberately maintained a relatively low-profile during Ted's prolonged absence, resisting the temptation to introduce any sweeping changes, I was mindful that the contents of this candid report would be seen as highly controversial in some quarters with it serving as a template for the many radical changes it advocated. The report, and its contents, were not entirely without a lot of support. In particular, two very key County Councillors, who would become my female 'political' bosses, welcomed it. Both women were Conservative County Councillors, representing the majority political group in power for much of the time I served in Dorset.

County Councillor Mrs Jenny Kellaway was in her late fifties and had been a fashion buyer in her former days and always looked immaculate in appearance. She was, by her own admission, a devoted follower of Margaret Thatcher and had a hairstyle not dissimilar, and she also loved wearing hats. Frequently controversial, she could be opinionated, combative and invariably very dominating. Despite her diminutive stature, she had a fearsome reputation, and it was a familiar sight to see very senior officers of the council running for cover whenever she was about. It was to my utter dismay to find she had just taken on the Chair of the Education Youth Service Sub-committee to whom I would ultimately report. But in spite of these earlier reservations, Jenny Kellaway would become one of the staunchest supporters and advocates of the youth service in the county. She was married to Stan, a very distinguished architect in

Poole. Much later in our relationship, Sally and I would be invited to her daughter Trina's wedding. Trina was a highly intelligent, vivacious, extremely caring women in her mid-20s, quite tall, attractive with vivid dark blond hair and brown eyes, with whom I would go on in the future to develop a strong close personal friendship.

County Councillor Mrs Pamela Seaton, who was Chair of the very powerful County Education Committee, was short in stature with dark features and hair, always beautifully coiffured, immaculate in appearance with her numerous twinset and pearls outfits, complemented by matching accessories. It was often remarked that she had a passing resemblance to the actress Patricia Routledge's 'Hyacinth Bucket' of the comedy television series 'Keeping Up Appearances', and Sally and I were often guests at one of her 'candlelit' suppers. Conversely, Pamela was always highly diplomatic, quietly spoken, exceedingly patient, understanding and very considerate, as well as respectful of others' views and opinions. Her husband, Peter, a quintessentially, courteous English gentleman in every sense of the word, ran a highly successful dental practice in Dorchester.

Conservatism was not the only common denominator that bonded them. Both had unswerving commitment, dedication and devotion to young people, especially those they considered in any way disadvantaged. Both played key and pivotal roles in the development of the Youth Service in Dorset and I would in time go on to form strong relationships with both. Many years later, both were to be awarded well-earned MBEs in recognition of their work with young people and Education Services.

In the meantime, news had come through that Ted had successfully applied for early retirement on medical grounds, with the support of his doctor. John Cooper decided that the post should be openly advertised, and it was a strategic decision that I fully supported. I was convinced that if I was going to bring about the dramatic changes I had envisaged for the service, I wanted to do this in the full knowledge that I had competed for the position and not automatically been handed it on a plate, as I never regarded myself as the 'anointed' one!

A month later, the interviews took place and despite a strong field of high calibre candidates from many parts of the country, it seemed I had impressed both Officers and Councillors during the interregnum period, especially the Deputy Education Officer, Richard Ely, and they had confidence in offering me the post of County Youth Officer. My second stroke of good fortune. But I knew this news would set off alarm bells in some quarters with a minority of protagonists who had made an unsuccessful effort to hijack my appointment.

Sally was delighted on hearing the news and resigned from her post in Southend, putting her house on the market which quickly sold, as did my property. The joint equities allowed us to have sufficient deposit to purchase an impressive Victorian-styled four-bedroom detached house near Dorchester. Soon after Sally had joined me, she was appointed to a full-time job in a commercial Training Agency in Weymouth.

It was very clear to me quite early on in my new position, that Richard Ely, the Deputy Head of the Department, not only had a very 'hands on' interest but was also a strong supporter of the Youth Service. An exceptionally intelligent, degree-educated individual, Richard was in his late forties, a quite tall, handsome man with a somewhat fresh, young-looking facial appearance, although possessing prematurely grey hair. During those early days, it was reassuring for me, with the sweeping changes that I had intended to implement, that I could rely fully on his support.

Within the first 12 months, I was able to introduce a number of professional changes, most importantly arranging early retirement packages for the ageing Youth Officers and replaced by a very competent and highly talented team of tenacious individuals, including three women. Many of these post-holders would themselves go on ultimately to secure very senior posts in other counties, as well as UK national positions. With the support of the Education Committee, I was able to implement a re-organised officer structure that allowed me to create a Deputy post, in addition to two County Assistants, each with operational responsibility for the East and West of the County, respectively.

These fundamental changes coincided with the establishment of a new independent Service Headquarters in a building block close to Dorchester station, giving additional impetus to the changes as well as enhanced service identity. Headquarters administrative staff had also grown in number, including one key appointment of the senior post of Strategy and Policy Development.

Of all the candidates interviewed, one stood head and shoulders above the rest. A young, good-looking man in his mid 20s, who was already working in the Education

Department, Anthony May. He would remain with me throughout my ten years with the service and in many ways serve as my 'gatekeeper' as well as becoming my right hand over that time, with me playing the role of mentor. A dedicated, highly intelligent, hard-working and loyal colleague who was a quite brilliant strategist. It came as no surprise to me to learn that 25 years later he had gone on to be appointed to the highest-ranking post in Local Government as Chief Executive of a very substantial cosmopolitan area in the Midlands. A genuine testament to meritocracy.

Very soon the new officer team were bringing about transformative and bold changes; a crucible for forging new ideas and values and the creation of a more cohesive service. Significant rises in youth centre membership and a cultural shift in accountability and transparency brought about tangible benefits. Communication and regular dialogue were also paramount to this progress with staff seminars held regularly, together with an annual staff residential conference to which prominent outside speakers were invited and a social evening for workers and their partners.

As acknowledgement of my previous experience in Essex and to Eric Hopwood, the service embarked upon an extensive programme of events and county-wide activities, generating new experiences and opportunities for young people and becoming a vital component and *raison d'etre* of the service; a period of frenetic activity with talent contests, disco dance competitions, quiz events, Youth Spectaculars (five were staged during my time, raising significant sums for local charities, including an HIV/Aids refuge in Bournemouth), were all part of a host of activities on offer.

There were, however, still challenges to be overcome with a minority of workers playing lip-service to empowerment and equal opportunities. I was nevertheless fortunate to have strong support from the voluntary sector, especially Peter Cunningham, who was Director of the Poole and Dorset Sailing and Activity Centre, with me eventually serving on its board of directors. Peter had been awarded an MBE in recognition of his services whilst working for the Boys Club movement in London, a few years earlier.

A 'watershed' moment for the service came with a call from the Lord Lieutenant of Dorset, Lord Digby, who rang to confirm that HRH Prince Edward had agreed to accept the invitation of Sherborne's Management Committee to officially open their new youth centre, recently completed with the support of a great deal of local fundraising and County Council. However, the Prince wanted to make this a whole day and evening visit and wondered if the service could organise events in relation to the Duke of Edinburgh Award Scheme (D of E) as he was now gradually taking a more prominent role in view of his father's advancing years.

Naturally, I was delighted by this unexpected news and the future implications this could have for the service in terms of prestige and prominence, and potentially my third element of good fortune. Also, on a personal level, giving me yet a further opportunity to become familiar with another member of the Royal Family! I asked Lord Digby to give me a few days to consult with the Chief Executive of the County Council, Mr Kenneth Able, and with colleagues and members of the voluntary sector. Also, with a very talented group of officers who had heralded in a tremendous amount of change already into the service, I felt very confident that we would be able to devise a full programme for that day and evening.

A week later I spoke to Lord Digby with our proposals outlining a very full and action-packed programme for the visit. Following the official opening of the Sherborne Youth Centre, the Prince would proceed to the Eastern conurbation of the County, Poole Park, where, accompanied by myself, he would then embark upon a Royal 'walkabout', seeing hundreds of young people from youth centres and clubs across the county engaged in a host of activities and events, particularly those of a D of E nature, many under colourful circus-type marquees, including a fashion show, creative arts area and musical concert, together with a huge outdoor skateboard display, assault course and a fancy dress Dragon Boat competition on the nearby lake. The whole area to be decorated with colourful bunting and flags.

This would be followed in the late afternoon by a black-tie and dress champagne and canapés event with musical accompaniment, in a banqueting room at a nearby five-star hotel in Bournemouth to which about 100 people would be invited with each paying £10 a head, with the proceeds being donated to the D of E Award Scheme. At its conclusion, the Prince would then proceed to the Pavilion (a thousand seat Theatre in Bournemouth) where he would attend a Youth Spectacular show performance of talented young people drawn from youth centres and schools in Dorset.

Lord Digby seemed delighted by our plans and agreed to consult Buckingham Palace and a week later we got the go-ahead. We were also very fortunate in finding a local benefactor who donated £5,000 to sponsor many of these ambitious plans, initiated by one of my "If you don't bloody well ask" moments!

Come the day itself, the Prince arrived on a helicopter of the Queen's Flight in an adjacent field marked out for the landing and was given an escorted tour of the Centre by the Leader and members of the Centre's Youth Committee. The Prince, accompanied by his Equerry, representatives of the National D of E Award Office and me then took a twenty-minute helicopter flight to Poole Park. The first, and last time, I would experience a memorable helicopter journey of the Queen's Flight!

Any suppressed excitement, however, was tinged with some degree of anxiety, as we were unable to forecast with any certainty just how many people would turn up for the event, in spite of the extensive local newspaper coverage. As the helicopter flew over Poole Park and before descending, the craft slightly tilted to one side and the Prince and other members on board gazed out of the windows to see Poole Park jam-packed with thousands of people. Despite overcast weather, the rest of the afternoon went off as planned, exceeding all our expectations. Because of the tight schedule on that day, it was necessary for me occasionally to move the Prince on to the next event, provoking at one stage a message being passed up the line to me: "Mr Palmer, please refrain from touching the Royal Personage!"

Following the hotel reception, superbly organised by Anthony May, the Youth Spectacular Show in the evening with a full house certainly represented the cherry on the cake, featuring many accomplished acts, including the highly talented Weymouth

Operative Workshop group of young people, under its Director and founder, Janet Stockley, who performed an impressive extract from the musical 'West Side Story'. The highlight of the evening concluding with a rousing chorus of 'Land of Hope and Glory' magnificently played by the Dorset Youth Orchestra, with all 200 cast members on the stage bursting their lungs and set against a backcloth of hanging Union Jacks with a pyrotechnic display to bring a climax to the show.

Prince Edward (who was seated next to me, along with other dignitaries in a reserved front row in the balcony of the theatre), was the first on his feet to join in a standing ovation at the conclusion of the show. He then went backstage to meet the cast and be presented with a commemorative plaque. At the final line-up in the theatre's foyer, it was very clear that the Prince had enjoyed his day with us, and the Chief Executive of the County Council gave me the unmistakable 'thumps up' sign.

The day had been a resounding success with many weeks of hard work coming to a successful fruition. County Councillors, as well as several colleagues from across the Department who had been invited, declared themselves very impressed by the events of the day and somewhat astonished that a relatively small service could pull off such a collection of prestigious events and in many ways a 'masterclass' in organisation. It was very flattering to be regarded by many County Councillors from then onwards as: 'The Jewel in the Education Service Crown'. In so many ways this was a game-changer for the service, especially as youth services, nationally, were generally regarded as the 'Cinderella' of Education Departments. However, I was keenly aware that none of this could have been possible without the full support of the very talented officer team, youth workers and voluntary sector and that a true spirit of *'esprit de corps'* made this possible. But I think we would have been forgiven for taking a brief victory lap, following that momentous day. The event also attracted widespread national, as well as local, television and media coverage, raising the profile of the Service in both the County and Region.

A year later I got a similar call from the Lord Lieutenant saying that Prince Edward was visiting the County again to open a new factory in Poole in the morning and had wondered if the Youth Service could arrange something in the afternoon. His visit synchronised perfectly with the completion of a newly built youth centre in Muscliffe, Bournemouth, and arrangements were put in hand for Prince Edward to officially open the new £250,000 centre and be given an escorted tour by youth centre members and to cut a commemorative cake. On the day itself, I was quite flattered that the Prince had remembered me from his earlier visit to the County and actually addressed me as "Bill".

Over the next five years, the Service grew exponentially, embracing a number of pioneering developments. The establishment of two drop-in Youth Advice Centres; launching a county-wide programme of sports and artistic activities; the purchase of a second-hand double-decker that was converted and used as a mobile Youth Centre visiting isolated village communities in the West of the County; two further visits to India in support of the Lotus Children Charity, raising an additional £25,000; undertaking two performing arts tours in Portugal and Uganda; staging the first Youth Environmental Awareness Residential with a representative group of five young

NEW BROOM THAT SWEEPS CLEAN

people from every European Union country; launching one of the biggest International Programmes (with financial support from the Commonwealth Youth Exchange) that included youth exchanges to every EU country, and first ever exchanges with Latvia, Hong Kong and the Gambia as well as visits to the USA and Canada, and a youth exchange with New Zealand to commemorate the 40th Anniversary of the Duke of Edinburgh Award Scheme and the running of two highly successful 'Question Time' type events, involving local politicians and young people. Over that period the Outreach and Detached Worker responsibilities in the County were also redefined, achieving enhanced accountability and transparency.

With the support of my Department colleague Len Saunders, who was the senior officer responsible for the Education Department's building programme, an ex-naval commander and very much an 'action speaks louder than words' kind of character and good supporter of the youth service, four new youth centre buildings were constructed, each designed following consultation with young people and incorporating 'special needs' facilities. Additionally, two centres underwent major renovation, and in addition, investment into a re-decoration programme for all centres in the county. This expenditure was 'ring-fenced' during a time of severe local government cutbacks.

Over the following two years, my 'Royal' calendar was quite busy, attending two Buckingham Palace Garden Parties in the presence of HRH Prince Phillip and Prince Edward to celebrate the D of E Award Scheme, and a reception at the Headquarters of the Commonwealth Youth Exchange, in recognition of the extensive overseas programme we were conducting, where I was personally introduced to the Queen and Prince Phillip. Following this, I was often the butt of Education Department colleagues' jokes with: "When are you expecting to be 'hob-knobbing' with Royalty again", and "By the way, Bill, when are you having afternoon tea at Buckingham Palace with the Queen? Any news yet?".

Throughout my Youth Service career, I had always laid great emphasis on Inter-Agency and Inter-Departmental links and co-operation. Over my tenure in Dorset, we established collaborative and strong links with the Police, Social Services, Probation, and Charities like the Prince's Trust, Commonwealth Youth Exchange, Children's Society and PHAB (the Physically Handicapped and Able-Bodied Charity) and many others, with whom we developed joint arrangements in terms of young people's provision.

I had, in particular, established an excellent relationship with the then Police Chief Constable of Dorset, Dick Aldous. He, together with his wife, had attended many of the high profile and prestigious events that we had organised. Also, to get a better understanding of the Service, he kindly took time out from his busy schedule to join me one evening to visit a few of the youth centres in the County. It was certainly my good fortune to have Dick Aldous in the County during my time, a man of considerable humility with a very keen interest in young people's welfare.

On the domestic front, Sally and I were continuing to pursue an active lifestyle and it was customary for us to take regular holiday breaks to ease some of the professional pressures. It was on one, a Far East tour, staying en route in Hong Kong, that I once again, started to seriously question my sexuality, finding myself inexplicably attracted to Asian men, but chose to keep those thoughts to myself.

Sally in the meantime had settled into her new job and was enjoying it, although finding its commercial environment quite demanding; she often felt that many Local Government workers did not always appreciate how 'feather-bedded' they were. Certainly, a rude awakening for me later in life! Whilst Sally took a yoga class each week, I continued to pursue my thespian interests, getting involved with a drama society in Weymouth and on one occasion being cast as an 'ugly' sister in the Pantomime 'Cinderella'. Some colleagues who attended the performance wryly remarked that my casting was a case of 'by name and nature'. Sally and I both had a passion for performing arts and made several trips to the beautiful city of Bath to take in a performance at the local Royal Theatre. We had by now furnished the house with beautiful items and were regularly hosting dinner parties for friends as well as family and thus enjoying a very comfortable lifestyle.

It was with immense personal sadness, after returning from one of our overseas holidays, to learn news that Barney Carlton, who still in his fifties, had suffered a massive heart attack from which he had not recovered. Barney would always be remembered by me as a truly kind, compassionate and caring person, who contributed so much to shaping my own professional development.

On a few occasions, Sally and I had discussed the possibility of starting a family, but with virtually two grown up children from her first marriage, I felt it would be unfair to her. As events were to unfold, this was a very wise decision.

With the Thatcher Government in its second term, considerable attention was now being focussed on Local Government and a demand for greater accountability and transparency. Along with this call for more openness was a diminution in the role of Local Education Authorities in relation to Further Education and direct control over schools and colleges. These devolved powers giving schools and colleges considerable independence.

The implications of such a policy resulted in the post John Cooper held being abolished, following his retirement. It also saw Richard Ely taking over as County Education Officer, following his predecessor's retirement, but the Deputy post eliminated as a result of Local Government cutbacks. In response to all these changes, the Library Service, previously a 'stand-alone' Service, was now to be merged into the Education Department – a move that several interpreted as bolstering the Department in response to its diminished central control. Consequently, the Careers Service, Adult Education, Library Service and the Youth Service were the few remaining 'direct' provision services in the Department.

These conspicuous changes brought about significant benefits and to the very pinnacle of my own career success. With the sanctioning of the Education Committee and Richard Ely, the Service was re-titled, 'Youth & Community Services' and my own title changed to that of 'Head of Service'. These quite seismic developments elevated me effectively to a second-tier officer status (two rungs up the pecking order), but also serving on the Department's Education Management Team.

Whilst Richard Ely, now heading up the restructured Department, and I had very contrasting personalities, almost 'chalk to cheese', we nevertheless shared a very fruitful relationship. I often felt, however, he regarded my matching tie and top suit pocket handkerchief as a rather 'flamboyant' display, almost in keeping with my 'risk-taking' and somewhat 'cavalier' working style. Despite a very busy schedule, Richard always took time out to accompany me around some of the youth centres every three or four months.

Throughout a plethora of change within our service, Richard, who generally adopted a more pragmatic management style, remained totally supportive and that was particularly crucial at a time when the Council were calling for deep cuts in some services, yet the youth service remained almost unscathed. This was also a period when other youth services, nationally, were taking massive cuts, resulting in full-time youth worker redundancies.

Following a visit to South America, the Prime Minister at that time, John Major, had expressed his genuine concern about the many street children he has witnessed on his visit, and had subsequently decided to host a reception at Number Ten for Charities involved in the work and Celebrities who shared his concerns. In due course, the Lotus Children Charity received an invitation from John Major, and they asked me if I would represent them at the reception, which I was very honoured to do. On the day itself, I travelled up to London in the late afternoon, taking a bus that dropped me off in Whitehall, close to Downing Street. Whilst I was making my way on foot up to Number 10, a stream of chauffeur-driven luxury cars passed me by, taking celebrities like Joan Collins and Terry Waite to the same destination.

Crossing over the threshold of Number Ten Downing Street was one of the most extraordinarily unforgettable memories of my life. Within a few minutes, I was being ushered up the famous staircase with framed photographs of former Prime Ministers hanging on the walls. As I proceeded up the stairway to be introduced to John Major, I heard a very familiar Scottish accent behind me. It was John Smith, Leader of the Labour opposition, who many considered at the time to be the 'Prime Minister in Waiting'. In the brief time we had to chat, I found he was a most unassuming, yet engaging man, and it was therefore a very poignant and sad moment when just two weeks later, news of his sudden death from a massive heart attack reached me, along with the rest of the world. I often reflected on how things might have developed had he become the future Prime Minister, although his successor, when in Government, would go on to introduce much-needed transformative change to the country over the next ten years.

One particularly busy morning in the office, I could see through the glass partition door that separated me from the outer office, an extremely tall, handsome man, with an incredibly athletic physique, whom I surmised to be in his mid-thirties, engaged in conversation with Anthony. Shortly afterwards, Anthony came into my office to inform me that the person in question had apologised for not making an appointment, but on the spur of the moment whilst passing the office, wondered if it were possible that I might give him a few minutes of my time.

This person was Junior Jones. He would go on to be one of the most dynamic people I had ever met up to that point in my life, ultimately becoming a very good personal friend, along with his beautiful wife Rachel and two daughters. It was another one of those times when the benefits of my 'open door' policy would pay amazing dividends and become another 'gold dust' find.

As a predominately 'rural' county, it was almost rare ever to meet someone from an ethnic background – although Junior was a British-born second-generation person, his family roots were originally in the Caribbean. Within the first few minutes of conversation, it became abundantly clear to me that any thoughts I might have entertained of returning to the 'urgent' work I was undertaking, were completely abandoned.

Junior Jones was a professional choreographer and dancer and was attempting to establish a foothold in the County with a view to working primarily with young people, especially those he considered disadvantaged. He was one of the most charming men I had ever met and his effervescent, extrovert personality were equally matched by his very disarming smile and dazzling white teeth.

After a long conversation, which continued over lunch, I agreed to launch a pilot scheme of evening dance sessions in a few of our youth centres with Junior as its choreographer. As always, Anthony was able to find a suitable budget heading and we mutually agreed to set-up a contract for a three-month trial period. Within a month, working in a number of the more disadvantaged areas of the county and with potentially challenging and alienated young people, using dance (primarily disco dance) as a medium to develop individual confidence and self-esteem, and in the process transforming individual outlook and attitudes, Junior, a consummate and very enlightened professional, became a runaway success story.

As a direct consequence of Junior's work, this was extended to other youth centres and a highly successful County-wide Disco Dance Competition was launched and incorporated in the Events Calendar, bringing together hundreds of young people to compete in area knockout heats before a Grand Finale. Junior's reputation soon gained hold and within a month his dancing expertise and young people's skill had been recognised and included in the curriculum of several schools. Junior would continue his close association with the Service, taking a lead artistic role in a performing arts tour in Uganda a few months later.

All these developments attracted attention from Her Majesty's Inspectorate in London, and we were subsequently approached with a view to a county-wide review of the Service in Dorset which was agreed. I was very confident that the vast number of changes that had been implemented over the preceding years, and strongly reinforced by our mission statement of empowerment of young people and equality of opportunity, would hold us all in good stead.

A few months later, three Officers from the Inspectorate undertook a one-month review of the service, involving personal interviews, visits, group discussion and questionnaires. Two months later their findings were published and made public. The report represented something of a 'poisoned chalice' for me professionally, and my personal nadir.

The Inspectors gave a 'glowing' report about Youth Service provision in Dorset and how impressed they were by the level of active involvement of young people in decision-making and general empowerment, and the service's commitment to equal opportunities. Overall, the report itself was a vindication of the very hard work and effort contributed by so many, and it was especially praiseworthy of the administration of the service, headed up by Anthony May.

There was, however, an ominous 'sting in the tail'. In spite of rating the service almost 100% in terms of achievement, viewing many as cutting edge developments, the report highlighted that the Inspectors had perceived me, based upon observations, as a somewhat autocratic Head of Service and not always adopting a consultative style of management, and thus seeing me as a 'lightning rod' for such observations. Criticism that I felt completely contrary to overwhelming empirical evidence.

Although profoundly shocked by the findings and trenchant critique, I was acutely aware that there were still pockets of resistance and dissenting views. However, Richard Ely and County Councillors, especially Kellaway and Seaton, were very upset by the comments and considered them a 'slight' on my professional character and reputation and felt compelled to write and express their dissatisfaction. I was nevertheless content to have any response 'kicked into the long grass', feeling that overall, the Service had been given the recognition it deserved, and a worthy reflection of the hard work contributed by so many. For me, however, both personally and professionally, it represented a 'Sword of Damocles' moment and a somewhat harsh penalty for ushering in what I instinctively and genuinely felt were long overdue reforms.

This report did also come at a very inopportune time for me personally. My marriage was now under considerable stress, especially as the County Council was going through a period of re-organisation with the Boroughs of Bournemouth and Poole becoming future Unitary Authorities, changes that represented an increasingly heavy workload.

Once again, over this period, I was also beginning to question my own sexuality, although I did not share any of these inner most thoughts with Sally. Nevertheless, I confessed to her that I did not feel I could go on any longer with our relationship. Understandably, Sally was devastated and shocked by this news, feeling utterly betrayed. Soon after she resigned from her training job and left the matrimonial home to re-join her family back in Essex.

For the next two years, Sally lived in Essex with her family where she was able also to secure a good full-time post, but throughout this period made no financial contribution to the household budget, intermittently making weekend visits back to the home. As a final attempt at reconciliation, we took a short holiday together, but I returned more convinced than ever that it was better to pursue a divorce settlement.

At the beginning of the third year, Sally returned to the matrimonial home, with the situation becoming increasingly intense, having given up her full-time job in Essex and taken a temporary full-time, lowly paid position with the local Council. Even at that point, I had not discussed with her in an open or honest way about the 'gay' feelings I harboured, having not been involved in any sexual relationships with men.

We both sought out respective Solicitors, but due to her changed circumstances, Sally qualified for legal aid, whereas, despite facing a mountain of debts, having maintained the matrimonial home for two years, without any support, I had no option other than to engage a solicitor, based in Dorchester.

Conscious that the path ahead, professionally, was strewn with uncertainty, given Local Government re-organisation on the horizon and the serious impact this may have upon Dorset, I applied for a national post as Chief Executive of Youth Clubs UK, based in London. Such a move would have elevated me into a very high-profile national position and onto a salary almost double what I was earning at the time. The post attracted a very wide selection of extremely experienced candidates from all parts of the country as well as different allied professions, but I was fortunate to be included in the short-list for interview.

Over a two-day interview process in London, I was finally selected with just one other candidate, who was already the Deputy CEO within the organisation, for the final round of interviews. Whilst I genuinely felt I had conducted myself better than any other previous career interview I had given, I was finally pipped at the post and the position was offered to the deputy. As developments would transpire, this would be the last 'throw of the dice' for me in terms of my professional youth service career.

A few months later, the Authority had broken up, leaving the newly created Dorset County Council with just the 'rural hinterland' and coastal area of Weymouth. In response to the first financial overview, the Service was now required to make cuts in provision and as other younger officers faced the real prospect of redundancy, including Anthony May, I decided to throw my hat into the ring and apply to Richard Ely for early retirement. It took several months of lobbying him and Councillors before it was reluctantly agreed.

This decision was also strongly motivated by the divorce proceedings, which had taken on a very acrimonious element and tone. My solicitor had advised me to move out of the matrimonial home, although I was still required to meet all the running costs of the house in Dorchester, including maintaining the mortgage and insurance payments as well as covering all utilities, and furthermore, to support Sally by paying £350 a month, whilst at the same time having to meet the rental of a small furnished flat I had found for myself in Bournemouth.

To overcome the crippling debts I was now incurring, including a loan from my niece Beverley, I felt my early retirement was an opportunity to seek a financial settlement and lasting resolution with Sally, who had engaged the services of a very 'combative' solicitor. Arrangements were therefore put in hand for me to secure an early retirement package, having completed 33 years in Local Government Service and a total of 36 years working with young people and the community. But I was convinced it was the best course of action to pursue under the circumstances, despite leaving a profession I absolutely loved.

NEW BROOM THAT SWEEPS CLEAN

Once agreed, I gradually started to withdraw to enable my successor, who was an internal appointment, time to get his feet under the table and to take over the reins. In the meantime, Anthony May was busy planning a farewell evening at a local youth centre near Dorchester.

At the farewell evening I was very flattered and honoured to have so many senior officers attend, as well as being able to invite several close friends, some of whom confessed to being surprised by the number of distinguished guests present including the Chief Constable, Chairman of the County Council and many others.

The evening was admirably and superbly organised by Anthony and took the form of a 'This is your life' format. The evening programme also included Weymouth Operative Workshop youngsters performing one of their impressive musical numbers – a group that had featured in every Youth Spectacular show we had staged, with by now my relationship with Director Janet, and husband John, developing into a close personal friendship. One man who seemed to be grinning with pride all evening was Eric Hopwood, who had taken the time and effort to drive from his home in Gloucestershire, to give a most touching and, at times, emotional tribute.

It was exceptionally sad for me to learn, when in Essex a few years later to visit my close friend, Debbie Holme, who had remained in touch with Eric, several years following his own retirement, he had succumbed to dementia and that the last time she had seen him, shortly before his death at aged 84, he looked very lonely and bent down sitting on a chair, totally bewildered and unable to recognise her. It was difficult comprehending that such an inspirational and dynamic person as EH, who had achieved so much for thousands of young people, should end his illustrious career and life in such a sad and tragic way.

Although the farewell evening would remain a cherished memory and a fantastic climax to virtually a life-time career in youth and community work, the report by the HMI Inspectors had hurt me personally and undermined my reputation and I genuinely felt had compromised any possible youth work legacy and the prospects of future freelance work within youth services. In some respects it represented a somewhat ignominious end to my career.

In the early summer of 1998, now 55, I found myself at yet another 'crossroads' in my life, my 'wings clipped', facing a precarious and uncertain future ahead of me. A time when the situation between Sally and myself and our respective solicitors, had become increasingly bitter and acrimonious.

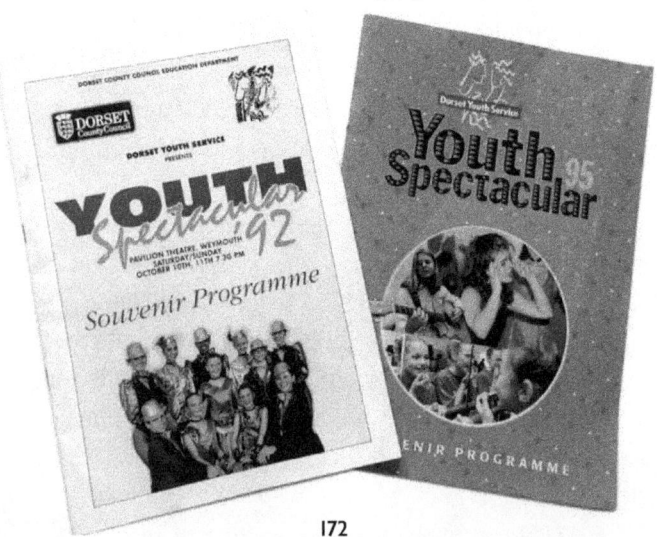

SOD'S LAW

Following my wonderful farewell evening, I was still living in my small, rented flat in Bournemouth, yet at the same time supporting Sally who was still working full-time. Although the *degree nisi* had been granted a year earlier, in January 1997, it would take another 18 months before a final financial settlement would be agreed, but in the meantime my debts were growing by the day. Sally's female solicitor was very competent, whereas I had come to the firm conclusion that my own solicitor was just about capable of house conveyancing, but otherwise totally out of his depth. He would continually advise me to respond to yet another vexatious affidavit, portraying me as some kind of wild, impulsive, 'money no object' character, only to add yet a further thousand pounds to his bill. I eventually took the decision to take things into my own hands and dispensed with his services, only to receive a final bill a week later for over £12,000!

Despite the heavy debts I was incurring, I knew that very soon I would receive my Teacher's Pensions lump sum, amounting to approximately £60,000. However, when I telephoned the Teachers' Pension Office to chase up the payment, I was informed that, under a new Government legal policy, any unresolved matrimonial disputes would have to be settled and, in the meantime, the amount had been 'frozen'. This action had been taken by Sally's solicitor who had alleged that I was a 'flight risk'. Eventually, after engaging another solicitor and barrister specifically, with a further bill of £3000, I was able to get the order overturned on the mutual understanding that a final settlement be agreed before a Presiding Circuit Judge in the County Court in Bournemouth in the late summer of 1998.

My niece Beverley kindly accompanied and supported me on the actual day of the Court hearing, knowing that I was conducting my own case, whereas Sally had both a Solicitor and Barrister to represent her. After a great deal of exchanges between both parties, the Judge withdrew and we were asked to wait until he was ready to give his verdict, having heard all the evidence submitted to him.

It seemed like an eternity before we were eventually invited back into the court room. In the Judge's summing up he was unambiguous that the settlement would be final, irrespective of any future financial change of circumstances by either party. After careful consideration, he had determined that Sally's legal submission of a lump sum payment of £40,000 and an additional £100 per month in perpetuity, was completely unreasonable. He had therefore decided that a one-off payment of £30,000 would be appropriate, given all the circumstances that had been submitted. He concluded by saying that his impression of Sally was of a woman he considered to be quite 'independent' and 'self-sufficient'. He then said he had found me a man of honesty, although somewhat 'mercurial'. I took this comment to be a reference to my 'gayness', which by that time I had openly declared.

Technically, this was a 'victory' for me, but a very 'bitter-sweet one', with Sally's legal team very shocked and surprised by the verdict. There were, however, really no 'victors' on that day, except what many had come to regard as the 'Merchants of Misery', the Barristers and Solicitors who take their inflated fees and move on.

Beverley was naturally very happy for me and wanted to celebrate afterwards, but I had just been through a heart-wrenching experience that had hurt me very deeply. Any slight happiness I might have allowed myself was overshadowed by genuine feelings of sadness, regret and guilt.

After one disastrous marital break-up, Sally had put all her trust and faith in me in the expectation that I would provide her with a secure and safe future. Her sense of betrayal was very understandable. For 11 years she had been a devoted and supportive wife and did not deserve the pain and suffering I knew I was now inflicting upon her. I was acutely aware that I would never atone for my actions. However, the court papers that were seen later did reveal that Sally had purchased a house in Witham, Essex and was back in full employment. Also, the financial amount that had been awarded to her in the settlement would be some compensation along with much of the house sale equity, as well as retaining most of the beautiful furniture and fittings from our home in Dorchester.

The balance from my Teacher's Pension Lump sum, following the settlement and payment of all my legal fees,

Credit Card and the debts I had incurred over the previous four years, left me with a paltry sum of £10,000. A sum of money that represented virtually a lifetime of work. Some friends observed at the time: "Wow, Bill. You really were taken to the cleaners". My response was quite simple: "Well, that's 'Sods Law'!"

It was a very high price to pay, financially, but my decision to declare myself openly 'gay' came with much more painful consequences. Very close friends, Nigel and Edwina, together with other mutual friends Sally and I had established over many years, totally cut me out of their lives and I never saw them again. Yet, as an indication of the kind of genuine people they truly were, Jenny Kellaway and Pamela Seaton and their respective husbands, continued to keep in touch and remained good friends.

After a lifetime, unconsciously in a state of 'denial', I could at long last be completely honest and true to myself and others, and for once in my life be totally free and uninhibited. The gay anthem by Gloria Gaynor: "I am what I am!" seemed to sum up perfectly my feelings at the time. I therefore had absolutely, *'Non, je ne regrette rien'*, about coming 'out' with my personal metaphasis now complete.

Nevertheless, I often wondered if perhaps I had been allowed, all those years earlier, to pursue a more artistic career path, rather than the educational one I eventually chose for myself, maybe my 'gayness' would have surfaced much sooner and thus, in consequence, avoiding a great deal of pain and distress. But, realistically, there would be many times over my lifetime when I would think to myself, "If only I had…!"

"ARE YOU BEING SERVED?"

Having reclaimed part of my equilibrium with the dust beginning to settle, I moved into a new flat in Bournemouth, having been able to secure a building society mortgage using my remaining lump sum as deposit. A delightful, small two-bedroomed flat that had been sympathetically converted within a Victorian styled house, very close to Meyrick Park in Bournemouth.

At the same time, I began forming a few gay friends through Lawrence, an interior designer by profession, a man I had met a few months earlier from a gay magazine advertisement (there being no such thing as websites like 'Trinder' or 'Grindr' in those days). A very handsome, intelligent and elegantly dressed person, in his mid-thirties, with whom I had established a plutonic relationship, Lawrence would eventually go on to live in Los Angeles. With his help, this very supportive group, although much younger, assisted me through my first tentative introductory steps into the local gay scene.

Meanwhile, it became manifestly clear to me that my modest monthly employment pension would be insufficient for me to maintain any prospect of a reasonable lifestyle, and therefore I started applying for various posts, emphasising what I felt were my 'transferable' skills. With many years being in the 'people' business and extensive travel, I approached Saga Holidays, an International Holiday Company in Kent, regarding any vacancies they may have for a rep's position. They responded, informing me that they had no positions at that particular time, but undertook to keep my name on their files and if any posts became available in the future they would get back in touch.

In the meantime, I made numerous applications to positions I felt were eminently suitable but was constantly being informed that I was too 'over-qualified'. Finally, a position became available of part-time Sales Assistant with Aquascutum, a quite 'high-end' menswear brand. Despite having no previous retail experience, I was still offered the job on a contract involving me working four hours every day over a six-day working week, knowing this extra revenue would ultimately make life much easier for me financially. The Company was a concession brand in a very large House of Fraser Department Store in the centre of Bournemouth.

The Manager of the Aquascutum store, Nigel, a man in his mid-forties, immaculately attired in his Aquascutum suit and accessories, was very approachable, possessing very good communication skills and well-honed customer service experience. He had a very gentle and sensitive nature and had clearly built up a good portfolio of clients over the many years he had worked for the Company, earning it a very good reputation locally for quality and classical tailoring.

Nigel was extremely patient with me in the first few weeks until I became more experienced on how generally to approach potential customers without appearing to be over intrusive. Nonetheless, being in the 'Are you being served?' environment felt strange and challenging for me, having previously been a Head of a Service with an annual budget of over three-million-pounds and responsibility for a staff team equivalent to 500 people. The expression "How the mighty are fallen" came to mind!

I was quite open about my 'gayness' and whilst I found this refreshing, I did not feel this in any way relevant. One day, however, I had cause to go into the store warehouse to collect a delivery of new items. As I entered, I overheard one of the store men announce rather loudly: "Watch out, boys, backs to the wall!" My almost instant response to this homophobic comment was: "Listen, boys, I may be gay, but I am not totally blind!"

Within the store there were a number of other 'concessions', including quite well-known brands. The Manager of the Concession next to our space was a very vivacious young woman, Michelle, who was in her mid-twenties, with striking, long flowing 'flame' ginger hair and was one of the most outgoing, gregarious persons I had ever met. Michelle, together with her future husband, Mike and two children, Sophie and Matthew, would go on to be very close life-long friends.

Michelle was a joy to be with and made periods of inactivity more tolerable. She immediately started calling me 'Billy', one of a string of nicknames I would acquire over my lifetime. There was, however, a price to pay for my relationship with Michelle, who was not only full of fun, but also a terrible prankster. One day when Nigel was having a morning off, unbeknown to me, she used the internal phone to call our department section, which I answered. Michelle pretended to be a female customer whom I had sold a pair of men's trousers to earlier in the morning. The person, sounding exceptionally upset, was shouting: "You sold me a pair of trousers I purchased for my husband earlier today, but you forgot to take off the security tag and when my husband struggled to remove this, he got squirted head to tail in blue dye. What are you going to do about it?" Full of apologies and doing my best to placate the woman, I suddenly looked across and saw Michelle laughing her head off and knew exactly who had been on the telephone. There would also be other occasions when returning from a short break, only to discover one of my display models with both arms missing – I didn't have to look far to know exactly who was responsible!

Michelle and me

I was very honoured a couple of years later, when asked to be one of her ushers at her marriage to Mike Hawkins (a delightful man, reserved and quiet and a perfect foil for Michelle) and given responsibility for handing out the floral buttonholes. A relatively simple task, but somehow, I ended up giving everyone the wrong buttonhole flowers. After the wedding ceremony, Michelle came up to me and jokingly said: "Bleeding hell, Billy, are you sure you were Head of a large Service? You can't even give the right buttonholes to everyone!"

Another good friend was Denise Van der Burg, who was Deputy Manager of Aquascutum Ladies Fashion.

Soon I was 'treading the boards' again, becoming very heavily involved with Bournemouth Little Theatre Club, a a very successful local am-dram group. Once again, as in my former days in Essex, participating in several Alan Ayckbourn plays. On a few occasions my good friends, Jenny and Stan Kellaway, John Richardson, and Suzi and John Grainger (both distinguished ex County Youth Officers) would attend to give me their support.

It had been about 40 years since my last visit to hospital, yet I would have three, almost simultaneous, encounters with Bournemouth's Royal Hospital, undergoing operations for a persistent abscess close to my anal entrance. It was only after the third operation that the situation was finally resolved. Some of my local friends observed, however, that I was something of a 'pain in the arse' and this seemed to confirm it!

Having felt from time to time down in the doldrums, over the second new year's holiday period I summoned up sufficient courage to take myself off on my own to a one-week exclusively 'gay' holiday in Gran Canaria – the very first time I had done this before in my life. This would not only be quite an 'eye opening' experience but where I would meet a gay couple who would also become life-long friends.

Once settled into one of the apartment flats that encompassed a large swimming pool area, I nervously made my way to the welcoming drinks area where other gay men were gathered. Here I met, for the first time, Andrew Macdonald and Glen Sheldon. They were both in their late twenties. Andrew was tall with short blond hair, deep blue eyes, very handsome with an alluring smile and personality to match. Glen was quite short, with handsome dark features, trimmed hair, quietly spoken and very articulate coming from a Jewish background. They were a monogamous couple and had been living together for about five years in Crouch End, North London and both accomplished professional classical musicians who played the violin.

I spent much of the holiday in their delightful company and each day we would head for the beach, surrounded by spectacular sand dunes. It was here that I was to have my first gay 'reality check' when discovering totally naked men walking brazenly about and where openly promiscuous behaviour was taking place between the dunes, and the men themselves!

One very extraordinarily special moment from that holiday that would remain forever embedded in my memory, was when Glen and Andrew, who had flown back with me to Heathrow Airport, came across to me (having collected their luggage at the carousel and exchanged addresses and telephone numbers), gave me a big bear hug and kiss. This was the first time in my life that anyone had done that to me publicly, let alone privately, and it gave me a wonderfully satisfying and "proud" feeling.

Andrew and Glen, the most caring and empathetic guys I had ever met, would go on to be very dear friends and it was my honour to be present at their Civil Ceremony Wedding in London many years later, joining them on that very special, joyful, and in many ways, historic day.

Periodic bouts of depression, bordering on bipolar, continued to plague me and one day Michelle mentioned to me that she had found a spiritual 'medium' in the town who had been very helpful to her. I was very sceptical, but eventually Michelle persuaded me to see the person, who lived in a small bungalow on the outskirts of town. On entering, I was led into a darkened room where there was just a table, upon which sat a glass of water, with two chairs either side.

Very soon a rather short man with a very distinct Irish accent entered the room, whom I had never met before. He proceeded to talk about my Mum, revealing intimate details only known to myself. Shortly afterwards, he suddenly stopped, informing me that another intermediary had just joined him in the spiritual world. Whilst the information he had already shared with me was quite compelling, I was not totally convinced. However, that feeling very quickly evaporated when he informed me that my dad was now present. After a few seconds, muttering under his breath, he suddenly said, "Your dad needs you to know that he is very proud of you and loves you for the person you are." It was something I had waited all my life to hear.

To help combat periods of depression, I joined a local David Lloyd Fitness Centre, and it was here that I first met my dear friend Sue Cross, who was the Restaurant Manager. Sue, a very attractive woman in her mid-forties, had a wonderfully positive outlook on life that inspired me to always look on the bright side, no matter my mood.

I was now enjoying a period of sustained stability in my life with my small apartment now fully furnished and began hosting a few dinner parties from time to time that close friends would affectionately christen 'Bill's M&S parties'. Apparently, I had a tendency to purchase a lot of food from that great store! This was not, however, to be confused with any sexual connotation of M&S!

Now feeling reasonably secure, financially, and having gathered around me a very close circle of friends, for some unfathomable reason I became restless and on the spur of the moment decided to approach a reputable exclusively gay hotel in Waikiki, Hawaii, with a proposition that for six months I would be prepared to offer my services, undertaking such tasks as administration or serving at table, in exchange for free board and lodging, but covering my own return flight fare.

Given my 'If you don't bloody well ask' mindset at that time, I nevertheless had very little expectation of a positive response. But two weeks later, I had an unexpected telephone call from the Manager of the gay 'Honolulu Hotel' taking up my offer, and we agreed there and then when I would fly to Honolulu. A month later, having resigned my part-time post and made arrangements with Michelle to care for my flat, and to the utter bewilderment of my many friends and family, I was off yet again in another direction, Pacific-bound.

HAWAII – OH! OH!

After a very long 20-hour flight, via San Francisco, eventually arriving at Honolulu Airport, I was met by a rather short, middle-aged Chinese man who introduced himself as Hui, informing me that he was the Manager of the hotel with whom I had spoken a few weeks earlier. I was never certain from then on, whether or not Hui was his forename or family name, but over my six months in Hawaii I always referred to him as 'Mr Hui'.

The Honolulu Hotel was situated in the middle of the beautiful, picturesque town of Waikiki. A well patronised exclusively gay hotel and the only one on the Island. It had ten 'themed' rooms including the 'Marilyn Monroe', 'New York' and 'Indian', with furnishings and décor mirroring their title. On entering the hotel, to the right of the reception, there was a partitioned off dining room area, serving small snacks at certain times of the day.

I fell immediately in love with Waikiki, it living up to its USP (Unique Selling Point). A combination of scrumptiously clean, pristine, pollution-free avenues with fashionable designer shops; an elongated paved promenade with golden sand beach leading to a turquoise Pacific Ocean – a utopia for surfers –swaying palm trees and at night the unmistakable sound of ukuleles playing in the distance. For me, it was pure bliss, although there were a minority who thought it too 'sanitised', like Singapore or Japan. But I felt it was the closest thing to heaven and a joy to walk down litter-free streets and not see buildings daubed with ugly graffiti.

Mr Hui, a somewhat enigmatic kind of man, reminded me of my earlier days with Hugh Dean. Very demanding, but always fair and I was allocated a good (non-themed) room and fed every day. He was also generous, giving me an additional $500 pocket money every month. However, I knew my visitor's visa would expire after six months and that my time in Hawaii would therefore be relatively short. I was also fully aware that the 'unofficial' working arrangement was actually quite unorthodox, as well as illegal!

My initial duties included staffing the reception area, and it was here that my earlier Pitman's typing skills were very helpful in coping with my first introduction to the hotel's computer. It was also the very first point of contact with the almost exclusively all-male guests and where again my earlier retail skills proved helpful. Occasionally, I would be asked to serve snacks in the nearby dining room area, but I was quickly called upon to use my creative skills and frequently tasked with decorating the roof garden of the hotel where 'unofficial' gay marriage ceremonies took place, although they had not been legally recognised at that time.

It soon became apparent to me that 'sexually' I had found my niche, as I was very drawn to Asian men who always 'floated my boat' from then onwards. Life in Waikiki soon, therefore, became very much a case of 'Hawaii, Oh! Oh!' with me pursuing a somewhat active gay lifestyle (almost as if I were catching up on lost time!). Within the first month I had already started a relationship with a young man, a twenty-four-year-old university student called Sang, from Seoul in South Korea, who was undertaking a post-graduate course, studying computer science. An exceptionally handsome young man, he would always insist on calling me 'William' (yet another nickname I was to add to my growing list). This casual relationship continued throughout my time in Waikiki, and we remained friends long after my departure.

Each morning I was normally assigned the early shift in the reception and every day around 8.30am passed by what I felt was a 'vision of loveliness'. This was Ines. She was in her late twenties, had long blond hair, blue eyes, fairly tall and had an amazing physique, was breathtakingly stunning with gregarious personality to match, and I was certainly instantly beguiled by her beauty. There was no mistaking the strong German accent as she would pass me each day with her morning greeting of "Aloha".

Ines had originally come from Hanover but on a holiday to Hawaii many years earlier, had met, fallen in love and married a local Polynesian guy, Henry. However, she soon became the victim of domestic abuse and had sought refuge in the hotel as a safe haven a few months earlier, whilst waiting for her divorce to be finalised. With the assistance of her cousin, already working in the hospitality business and who had connections with the Honolulu Hotel, she had been able to negotiate a relatively long stay arrangement in one of the themed rooms.

Ines was an exceptionally creative hair stylist who worked at a well-known hair salon on the island and her former marriage to Henry allowed her to acquire a 'green' card and to be awarded full USA citizenship.

Very soon we became close friends and almost from the beginning of our relationship, she would insist on calling me yet another sobriquet: 'Billy Boy'. Ines not only attended to my 'locks' regularly, but three times a week I would join her for a very early morning jogging session around the nearby local canal. She was also an accomplished tennis player and I was persuaded to join her from time to time, although I was not an aspiring 'Andre Agassi' and frequently she could be heard, on most occasions, shouting from the baseline: "Oh! Billy Boy, at least try returning the ball!"

A year after I had left Hawaii, Ines, following her divorce, returned to her home city of Hanover where she once again met and fell in love but with a young German guy in his late twenties, Timo, a man with an astonishing physique, resembling a young Arnold Schwarzenegger with typical Aryan German looks, with his blond hair and blue eyes. They eventually married and I visited them at their home in Germany two years later. But the overwhelming desire to be back on the sunshine island of Hawaii led them to return to Waikiki, where they bought an apartment and settled. Ines's citizen status eventually enabled Timo to gain a green card and full USA citizenship, and he subsequently went on to develop a career in printing and graphics, whereas Ines started her own hair creation salon.

Although my regular regime with Ines was helping me to stay in reasonable shape, I still nevertheless took out a temporary membership of a local 'Fitness First' Centre, attending generally three times a week. My usual exercises were taken in front of panelled glass windows where I could continually enjoy panoramic views of golden sand beaches, swaying palm trees and white horse waves rolling up from the Pacific Ocean. It was a joy and a far cry from Bournemouth.

My six months exiled on what I had come to regard as my temporary 'tropical paradise' island had quickly come and gone, and soon I was on the flight back home to the UK and Bournemouth. Though exhausted after my long flight, I knew that in my absence Michelle would have taken good care of my flat, but I was in for a total shock as I entered. It was festooned in streamers and balloons and silver stars fixed to the ceiling, but what took me by complete surprise, however, was that my arrival had somehow activated a china lobster sitting on my dining table, that immediately started humming a tune and waving his claws in time to the music. This was a typical 'Welcome Home, Billy' from Michelle!

Within a week, Nigel had offered me back my previous part-time post in Aquascutum, and I was soon into a familiar routine and sharing with colleagues my many anecdotal adventures in Waikiki. A few months later, however, in early 2000, Nigel found another position within the industry and the Area Manager of Aquascutum, Susan Augustus, offered the full-time position to me, which I accepted. Yet another new challenge, but with it a constant reminder that just a few metres away, Michelle would be 'keeping me on my toes!'.

A few weeks after my arrival home, the devastating and deadly terrorist attack on the Trade Centre twin towers in NYC, shook the whole world, and changed life for everyone from that moment onwards.

One day about a year later, and quite out of the blue, I received a letter with a Folkestone post-mark which would become a 'red letter' day for me. Its contents would open a new door for me and ultimately take me down a markedly different and unique pathway for the next 17 years, and onto the threshold of an exciting new career.

"CAN YOU HEAR ME AT THE BACK?"

I had been invited for interview at Saga Holidays Headquarters Office at their nerve centre in Folkestone in Kent. On the day itself there were about a dozen prospective candidates all gathered in what resembled an enormous inflated white marquee, that stood astride a large vertical transparent glass building settled on the top of a steep hill called Enbrook Park.

After group discussions and role-play sessions, I was very fortunate to be taken forward to the final interview. The key person on the interview panel was a good-looking woman whom I felt to be in her early forties, with striking blonde shoulder length hair and blue eyes with a hint of a Cockney accent. She was the Head of the Reps Department, Anna Collins.

Despite my obvious lack of any previous holiday industry experience, Anna said I had impressed the panel by my enthusiasm and commitment and that they were happy to offer me a position on the rep's team. Having had so many disappointments previously, I was naturally delighted by this and generally felt I was on the 'up and up' again. On my return to Bournemouth, I submitted my notice to Aquascutum, although this excitement, however, was slightly overshadowed with some apprehension, as there had been no guarantee of work and this had been made abundantly clear in the interview. Embarking for the very first time in my life into unknown territory and a freelance work environment, I began to seriously wonder if I had made the right decision.

My fears, however, were short-lived. About ten days later the familiar voice of Anna was on the 'phone to tell me she wanted me to go to Chiang Mai, a resort in Thailand, for two months and work at a hotel, The Imperial Mae Ping. Also, on my return, I was to assist on a two-week Mediterranean cruise on the 'Black Watch', a Fred. Olsen Cruise Line Ship. She also confirmed that my 'turquoise' jacket (the Company colour of Saga), shirts, trousers and personal mobile would also be sent to me.

This was perfectly synchronised with my notice to Aquascutum, yet I knew I would miss the many hard-working colleagues in the retail trade, whom I felt were often maligned as being unfriendly and unhelpful, completely contrary to what I had found. Michelle was away on maternity leave at that time and a month later gave birth to a son, Matthew. News I was overjoyed to hear.

I thoroughly enjoyed my time in Thailand, especially the local Thai people, and could quite understand why it was often fondly referred to as the 'Land of Smiles'. The cruise was also a totally new experience for me, and I was very fortunate to have an extremely attentive and supportive Cruise Manager, Elizabeth Halstead. It was also my good fortune to meet two delightful guests, Jan and John Daws, who not only shared our evening dinner table but some of my silly jokes. Over the years, both Jan, John and Elizabeth remained in touch with me.

With the completion of my first two assignments and some good feedback from clients, Anna offered me a six-month posting at a new resort in the Sinai desert, Egypt. Having felt that resort work was somewhat repetitive, I was not especially enamoured by the offer. Nevertheless, Anna convinced me that I was the right person to take on this exciting new bespoke project and assured me that the location of what she described as a magnificent five-star hotel, was very close to the Israeli border and the busy northern town of Eilat, and easily accessible during any leisure time periods. And her final words to me: "You're going to be our new 'Lawrence of Arabia', Bill!'" It seemed that in those early days, I bore a close resemblance to the famous and distinguished actor, Peter O'Toole!

Overnight en route to the Sinai, I stayed in Aqaba, Jordan, before taking the sea ferry across to the Port of Nuweiba, in the Sinai, where I was met by a very tall local Arab, Mouhamed (not exactly an 'Omar Sharif'), with the typical Arab greeting, "Salam", who took me by car to what was the magnificent five-star hotel, The Steigenberger. It certainly lived up to Anna's promise, but only for me to quickly discover that the hotel, with all its sumptuous facilities, was actually about 45 minutes' car drive from the town of Eilat!

The Manager of the Hotel was German, a very tall, slim and dark haired, quite distinguished man in his early forties but with a personality and temperament not that dissimilar to Basil Fawlty of 'Fawlty Towers' fame, (although I never actually ever saw Sybil). As I had anticipated, the six months were very repetitive and soon I had become all too familiar with each night's dinner menu. In spite of the drawbacks, the compensations included the generous warmth of the Egyptian staff and local guides. This also included the enthusiastic clients arriving twice a week, involving a 100-mile return bus journey to meet them at Sharm El Sheik Airport in the north, where I was often heard to say during my introduction on the bus: "Can you hear me at the back?".

Whilst the regular routine of excursions was keeping me fully occupied, I still found it a lonely and tedious posting and at the end of my six months, was happy to leave behind the barren sandy landscape, scorching heat and dromedary camels of the Sinai and relieved to see the cavalry arrive on the horizon in the form of Malcolm Fairman, my successor.

Towards the end of my somewhat prolonged stay, however, news came through that Anna Collins had decided to go back to becoming a long-haul Tour Manager and that a Makala Thomas was her replacement. Makala would go on to be my Line Manager for the next 16 years and over that time ensured I had a very generous allocation of tours, with the majority of my freelance work being principally long-haul assignments, including flag-ship tours to China. Throughout this time, Makala was very ably assisted by her extremely competent Administrative Assistant, Kylie Lodder.

I was quite surprised to discover very early on with the Company, that the idiosyncratic behaviour normally associated with young people, with whom I had worked previously, bore a striking similarity to Saga clients. However, all Saga clients were aged over 50 years and the Company's principal *raison d'etre* with this niche market age group, and one distinct characteristic was their self-deprecating sense of humour. When Saga was first formed in 1951, it was customary in those early days for clients to refer to the term Saga (although not an acronym) as 'Sex And Games Abroad' but later to become, 'Sex Annually Generally August', indicative of their very good sense of fun to the point of self-parody.

Occasionally, a client would comment on how wonderful it must be having a job where you were on holiday all the time, staying in beautiful hotels and doing that at someone else's expense. The majority of clients, however, did fully appreciate the onerous responsibility involved and the demands to be on call throughout the tour, dealing with sickness and other problems, and on most occasions leading a group of over 40 clients. Whilst no field staff member would underestimate the 'fringe' benefits, equally there would be times when you were called upon to deal with clients arriving on tour, unaccompanied and clearly suffering from acute dementia or incontinence.

When I first joined Saga in 2001, it was still a family-run business founded by Sidney de Haan. But as with many other companies, it developed into another very large Corporation, with an ethos driven by a much greater emphasis on financial imperatives and increased central control, leading to a change of status of field workers from freelance to self-employed. In spite of these changes, Saga Holidays remained one of the leading and most successful companies in the industry, operating in a very precarious and unpredictable global environment with increased terrorism, hurricanes and pandemics.

Much of the Company's success, however, could be attributed to the dedication and commitment of field staff (many of whom I had the privilege of working with and very proud to be part of such a dedicated team), who exercised amazing levels of 'duty of care', yet as self-employed workers were constantly required to work extraordinarily long hours with levels of pay lower than any other company in the industry, at the time, below the EU minimum wage. As a result, being excluded from accepted Employment benefits, yet continually subjected to arbitrary assessment through clients' questionnaires. Over my last four years with the Company, many very experienced field staff left, with some viewed by Saga as *'agents provocateurs'*, simply by raising legitimate concerns over basic employment rights that a few interpreted as bordering on exploitative.

Over my 17 years with Saga, I was recognised on a few occasions with five separate 'Achievement Awards', but these paled into insignificance compared to a colleague of mine, Di Keddie. A Scottish woman, in her late twenties with the, by now, Saga trademark long blonde hair and blue eyes, accompanied by a dazzling smile and infectious personality to match. Her *'Je ne sais quoi'* was self-evident to all who had the pleasure of meeting her.

Di was Saga's most outstanding and best Tour Manager and won numerous awards during her long association with the Company. I first met her when our respective tour groups coincided on a Yangtze River Cruise in China and for me, a fortunate stroke of serendipity. We became instant friends and remained so, and in the autumn of 2018, I had the pleasure of spending a brief time at her lovely home in the small village of Macduff, bordering the River Deveron estuary in Scotland.

Di and me

After four years working with Saga and living by now in Hong Kong, I was being allocated primarily Far East tours, particularly the three different tours operating in China. It was therefore quite a normal routine for me to take the three-hour flight by the airline Dragon Air, to Beijing, China's capital city, from Hong Kong. By that time, I had become increasingly aware of cultural differences, especially concerning humour, and this was dramatically illustrated one day when checking in for my flight. I made my customary request for a bulkhead or emergency aisle seat on account of my long legs and the young Chinese woman behind the counter was extremely helpful and immediately began exploring the possibility on her computer. Without much thought, I then made a rather stupid comment: "If you could do your best to get me an extra leg-room seat, I would be very grateful, as I have an appointment with a Beijing hospital to undergo an operation to have four inches taken off my legs, so I don't have this problem in the future". The reaction and response from the young woman was instantaneous: "Oh my goodness, will it hurt?" I then spent the next five minutes fruitlessly endeavouring to explain to her that it was a silly joke on my part, but she still persisted in expressing her genuine concern, and finally allocated me an emergency aisle seat on the flight. As I left, she called out after me: "Mr Palmer, please take care, and I hope the operation is successful".

Six years after joining Saga I had the privilege of being the first self-employed male worker to be offered two 'Around the World' Tours, each lasting 42 days and covering 30,000 air miles with 22 flights, internal and international, and 25 hotel stays. This was not only Saga's flagship tour, but one of its most expensive and requiring an enormous amount of preparation, as well as physical stamina. I was most fortunate, however, to have on both occasions, two exceptional groups who bonded very well with each other, as well as myself.

The tour included eight countries. One moment you were on safari in South Africa with intense 45-degree centigrade temperatures, the next in the Forbidden City, Beijing, experiencing sub-zero temperatures. Then just as quickly, back again into the searing heat, witnessing the majesty and wonder of the iconic Taj Mahal Temple in Agra, built to symbolise a Mughal Emperor's love and devotion to his wife. In India we stayed in a particularly sumptuous 6-star hotel, with butler service on each floor. The Indian guests included one owner of a gold-plated Rolls-Royce parked outside the chandeliered, thick-carpeted entrance lobby. Yet, paradoxically, within 500 metres of the hotel, we passed a group of destitute people sheltering in the street gutter. Such grotesque inequalities were commonplace and seemed utterly incongruous with a country possessing nuclear arms.

On the second tour, one client loomed larger than life itself, Jilly Nowell. A septuagenarian, she was rather short, silver-haired and a quite attractive, if not somewhat loquacious woman, who was always immaculately dressed. She looked remarkably younger and had the energy and vitality of a person half her age and an extraordinarily '*joie de vivre*', with a wonderful sense of humour and very generous. She loved to party and thoroughly enjoyed her favourite gin and tonic drink, enjoying the odd one or two 'tipples', following dinner.

Jilly and I got along famously, and it was on this tour that she adopted another nickname for me, 'Willy', and was the only client over my seventeen-year career with Saga who asked me outright if I was gay. Jilly and I remained very good friends and in 2017 she celebrated her ninetieth birthday, having recovered from bowel cancer a few years earlier, yet remaining as sprightly and as alert as ever and still indulging in her favourite 'tipple'.

Several clients would also go on to be good friends that I met initially on tours: Veronica Richardson on a Caribbean, Kathleen Titley on a Japan, Alan and Sue Coe on an Around the

World, Chris and Vince Gladwell (Vince being a horticultural expert who accompanied a group to Japan), and many more.

During one of my frequent flights to the UK at the beginning or end of a tour and whilst still living in Hong Kong, I would endeavour to visit my twin sister, Pam, and her husband Alf, who lived quite close to Gatwick Airport in Horley. Alf, a very large man, physically, had been forced to give up full-time work due to acute emphysema and was regularly receiving treatment at home and at the local hospital. On one quick overnight visit, I was privileged to sleep in their second bedroom, previously Gary's room, and still very much a shrine to his memory. As the evening progressed, Alf, who had been sitting in a chair watching television with us, suddenly slumped over, apparently having suffered a massive heart-attack and had stopped breathing. I managed to drag Alf off the chair and onto the floor and attempted to resuscitate him, whilst Pam called for the paramedics who arrived about ten minutes later.

With the help of a defibrillator, the paramedics managed to get Alf back to life and he was quickly rushed to the local hospital for emergency treatment. Although he regained consciousness, the lack of oxygen he suffered resulted in quite severe brain damage and after a few months he had a further heart attack from which he did not recover. Alf was also laid to rest at the Surrey and Sussex Crematorium where he would join his son Gary and my mum and dad. Pam was understandably very devastated by Alf's tragic death and I knew she would find life incredibly lonely after a long marriage of 50 years.

Very tragically, two years later, lightning struck again, when Pam was diagnosed, very unexpectedly, with ovarian cancer and had to undergo chemotherapy treatment for over a year, losing her hair and considerable weight in the process. It was a very distressing time for me, feeling so impotent, being many thousands of miles away, but comforted by the knowledge that she had the support of her immediate family, as well as some remarkably modern-day 'Good Samaritan' neighbours.

Very sadly, Pam eventually succumbed to the disease just over a year later and I was fortunate to be able see her in hospital for the very last time a few days before her tragic death. Somehow, she seemed resigned to her fate with her visibly skeletal appearance so indicative of the corrosive effects of the disease.

It was a tremendous honour for me to be asked to give a eulogy at her funeral, which was beautifully organised by her family. In my final tribute to Pam, I confessed that, unlike me, she did believe in a Heaven and that if, in my view, such a place did exist, I was totally convinced that this gentle, quiet, sensitive and beloved twin sister of mine would have already been fully embraced into the family of 'Angels'. It seemed highly appropriate that Pam too be cremated at the Surrey and Sussex Crematorium, thus joining the family.

In so many ways, it was quite poignant and rather surprising for the whole family to discover that after her death, Pam had left several thousand pounds for her son and daughter to inherit, yet she had always chosen to lead quite a frugal lifestyle. Somehow, I felt this action was strongly motivated and influenced by our own parents' passing.

Although the work of a Tour Manager could be very arduous and demanding, there were always lighter moments that made for very amusing anecdotes. Three of the most memorable for me were in China, the Caribbean and Japan.

Amy was a brilliant Chinese tour guide in Beijing, but having just spent a year undertaking an academic study to enable her to get her essential guiding credentials, this had to be followed up by a practical guiding session, her first group being American. In spite of being very fluent in English, Amy was quite apprehensive with this first group and her nervousness led her to inadvertently confusing her words. Whilst the group were passing through the Forbidden City and her talking about a certain Ming Dynasty Emperor, she referred to this ruler as having had over a hundred 'Cucumbers' when clearly she meant to say 'Concubines'. The American group's response, however, was: "My, he really loved his cucumbers!".

On a day visit to the island of Mustique (an island often associated with Princess Margaret), a somewhat voluptuous young Black African American woman called Molly, from New Jersey, asked if she could join our party for our return sea trip back to the island of Bequia, which I was happy to agree to. Molly was a wonderfully captivating person with a very outgoing personality and great sense of humour. In doing my best, somewhat nonchalantly, to assist her onto the boat, she somehow missed her footing, slipped and pulled us both into the water to the great amusement of clients who were watching this entire spectacle. It was especially embarrassing for me looking rather 'dandyish' in my Saga turquoise polo shirt and crisp white trousers at that time.

Most of the Japan tour involved clients on quite long coach journeys and these were always accompanied by very highly knowledgeable guides. One day when we were going through a mountain pass region, we suddenly spotted a group of monkeys ahead on the road, and I asked the guide what species they were, expecting her to say, Rhesus or Proboscis, yet her very prompt reply was simply "Japanese monkeys!".

It was very easy to become somewhat complacent and egotistical with many questionnaire responses from clients placing me in the top performing category. Just as I thought I was riding high, I was once brought down to earth with a bump when a rather difficult man on a China tour returned his questionnaire. As customary, this remained unopened and returned to Saga HQ. A few days later, Customer Services rang me to say that this particular client had rated me 'very poor' in every category (including appearance!) and added, "Bill Palmer must be Saga's worst Tour Manager. He had a mind of useless information!". Reassuringly, my manager confirmed that his questionnaire had found its way into the bin, as all the other members of the tour group had rated me 'excellent'. It was, nevertheless, a salutary lesson, never to assume or take anything for granted.

There was also one very brief moment when I thought I was going to fulfil my ambition of becoming famous. Saga had been approached by an Independent Television Documentary Group with a view to undertaking a pilot scheme involving filming a Resort Manager whilst working with clients. I was asked if I was interested in doing this, with the Company offering to pay for my air fare from Hong Kong to the stunningly beautiful, picturesque Italian island of Sorrento and stay at a magnificent five-star hotel where the filming would take place over two days. Without hesitation, I agreed immediately and within a couple of weeks found myself being filmed and directed enthusiastically by a very young female director who continuously assured me: "You're a natural, Bill, the camera loves you!". I was already beginning to have illusions of being the next 'Michael Palin'! Allegedly, the filming had gone extremely well, and everyone seemed very happy with the outcome, and I returned home thinking that my life was about to change irrevocably. My hopes were quickly dashed, however, when about a month later, Saga Headquarters rang to say that the film company had chosen to go for an Ocean Cruising documentary, as an alternative. So much for the camera!

Similarly, many, many years earlier, I thought I was going to have a life of fame and fortune when I had a very brief courtship with the glamourous world of male modelling. But after just one appearance in a national newspaper advertisement and two catwalks, I rapidly re-focussed my sights on a more promising career, having abruptly come to the conclusion that I was never going to make the neon billboards of New York Square.

Over my 17 globe-trotting years with Saga, I was privileged to visit over 60 countries, from such destinations as Oceania Australia to the archipelago island of Zanzibar, witnessing places and events that simply took my breath away. But more importantly, met some of the most incredibly interesting people from all walks of life: actors, poets, retired politicians, Lords of the Realm, authors, former television presenters, three sets of twins, four lesbian couples and two gay couples.

There were countless times when I felt I had the very best job in the world, yet other times when it was a case of, "Get me out of here, I'm a Saga Tour Manager!".

Me sitting on famous seat in front of Taj Mahal

LOVE IS SOMETIMES BLIND

After about my second year with Saga, having totally settled into my flat in Bournemouth and between tours, maintaining an active social life, especially with friends Michelle and Mike, who by that time had had their second child, Sophie, and now that my finances were on a more stable footing, I decided to take a short one-week holiday to Hong Kong, a country I had visited before and had always fascinated me, given also my attraction towards Asian men.

As a gay person, I never felt comfortable in bars or clubs, instead choosing to pursue possible contacts through the many gay websites that were by that time available world-wide. In advance of my visit, I had already arranged to meet a guy on the second night, following my arrival. An encounter that would ultimately go on to turn my life completely upside down.

The person I met was a man called Georges. When he first opened the door to his tiny apartment on the Hong Kong Island side, I was simply bowled over by the amazingly handsome man who stood before me. Georges was about 35 years old, Hong Kong Chinese, very fit with dark hair and matching eyes and as I was soon to discover, employed full time as an English teacher in a local secondary school.

It was a case of 'love at first sight' for us both in spite of the age differences, and we spent the rest of my brief holiday in each other's company. For me, this was the one ultimate relationship I had been waiting for all my life and someone with whom I would spend the rest of my days. I was totally and utterly besotted with him, and over the next four months I visited him five times, taking long weekend flights, the cost of which depleted most of my savings, staying each time with him in his tiny apartment. Georges, however, eventually persuaded me to relocate to Hong Kong so that we could share a life together, and eventually marry once Civil partnerships became legal. In the meantime, we exchanged Cartier silver engagement rings.

It was another of those moments in my life when I heard a different voice in my head, this time my mum. I made the fatal and impulsive decision to sell my flat and furnishings in Bournemouth so that we could have sufficient finances to support a reasonable lifestyle, as Georges was working full-time, and Makala had also confirmed that I could continue undertaking Far East tours.

Friends, as well as family, were delighted by my news but genuinely concerned that I was on the verge of taking a big step, but I was totally convinced that my future was secure. Three months later, having sold up, Georges and I set up home in a fairly large, three-bedroomed unfurnished apartment in a reasonably up-market part of Central Hong Kong, called Mid-Levels. We agreed to share the monthly rental, with me providing the substantial deposit from my flat sale equity, and also to purchase items and furniture for the new apartment.

I then embarked upon a somewhat reckless spending spree, funding three holidays that we took together over the next 12 months. Yet already I was becoming increasingly concerned with Georges' capricious and unpredictable mood swings; days when he would be overtly affectionate and others when he would completely ignore me. A virtual 'Jekyll and Hyde'. Of greater concern was that I had become convinced he was no longer upholding our monogamous relationship, especially when I was away on tour. At the start of our second year together, his continuing indifference towards me became even more distressing and he would continually dismiss my concerns, but unlike Georges, I was not fortunate to have a support network of family and friends locally.

It was during this time that my respiratory problems were giving me cause for concern, exacerbated by the high pollution levels in Hong Kong, so I sought medical advice. Dr Michael Lo, who had a surgery close by, was one of the most compassionate and caring doctors I had ever met, and I was able to freely talk openly with him about my gay relationship with Georges. He had been trained in the UK and for the first few years after qualifying, practised in a surgery in Yorkshire. Michael was a Hong Kong Chinese man in his mid-thirties, a highly intelligent person who had not only gained a Doctorate Degree but also went on to study and be awarded a Degree in Law.

Soon the situation between Georges and I had reached boiling point with the relationship haemorrhaging very rapidly.

Suddenly, one day, when confronted, he openly admitted that he was having other sexual relationships with men and wanted to end the relationship, confirming this the following morning by mobile text and a follow-up email. It was the lowest point in my life and a very sad denouement to what I had hoped to be a perfect long-term partnership. Whilst my immediate response was to escape from this desperate situation as soon as I could, I found myself in a Catch-22 situation, knowing that if I left prematurely, Georges could conceivably withhold the considerable cash deposit I had put down to secure the flat. Thus, I was stranded for a further two months.

The acute depression, sense of loneliness and isolation I was feeling drove me once more back to see Dr Michael for treatment. I explained to him about the impending break up and how I had trusted Georges sufficiently to engage in unprotected sex with him in the latter stages of our relationship. As a cautionary measure, he suggested I should undergo an HIV test and he took a blood sample and sent this to a laboratory for an analysis. As soon as I walked into Michael's surgery a few days later, his demeanour suggested immediately all was not well. "I ran two tests, Bill, the second at my own expense, and I very much regret to have to tell you that the results have come back confirming you are HIV positive. I am dreadfully sorry to have to give you this terrible news."

It was one of the most devastating blows of my life, almost as if I were being served a death penalty, thinking I would go on to develop full blown Aids. Michael referred me to a local hospital, but as I did not enjoy Right of Abode status they refused me any treatment. I had no alternative but to make plans, as soon as I could, to return back to Bournemouth and seek treatment at the Royal Hospital where there was a men's health clinic.

Having not engaged in any form of unprotected sex with anyone prior to Georges, I knew he could only be the one who had infected me, and I was soon to discover that he had a very notorious reputation locally, tantamount to a sexual predator. When I finally confronted him, he completely refused to accept it could have been him that had infected me with this life-threatening disease and dismissed any suggestions that he too be tested. It was almost as if it was just a calculated and callous game of Russian Roulette to him.

My diagnosis was something I felt I couldn't share with anyone. I felt unclean, a tremendous sense of self-loathing and thoroughly disgusted with myself, made worse by the knowledge that in my former profession, I had been a very strong advocate of sex education. It was a moment of horrendous despair. Each day my mounting depression gave rise to serious thoughts of suicide, the stigmatisation of HIV/Aids casting a long, dark shadow. Eventually, I summed up enough courage to share this news with my two gay friends, Glen and Andrew, back in England, knowing they would fully understand and be supportive. As I had anticipated, they were completely non-judgemental, advising me to seek help as soon as possible at the clinic in Bournemouth's Royal Hospital and giving me details about the Terrence Higgins Trust where I could also seek additional support. This was very typical of their amazing kindness and for me, a much-needed indispensable lifeline. However, it would be many years later before I had sufficient courage to share this intimate knowledge with other close friends, and especially some members of my own family.

I was extremely fortunate to have a very good friend, Karl, in Bournemouth, whom I had worked with previously when in the retail trade. He and his partner, Mike, had a large modern house near the centre with a self-contained flat in the basement that they were happy for me to rent, saying I could stay there for as long as I needed. I was also lucky to be able to continue my work with Saga, which actually opened up more tour opportunities for me. However, before leaving Hong Kong, I vowed that I would never allow myself to ever become intimately involved with another man, coming to the ultimate conclusion that 'my love had been blind'. I wondered also, if in some strange way, this was a form of divine intervention for the pain I had put Sally through many years earlier.

It seemed like an eternity before eventually I was on my way to the airport for my flight back to England. There were going to be so many aspects of Hong Kong life that I knew I would really miss, in spite all the intense personal pain associated with it.

ALL THAT GLITTERS IS NOT NECESSARILY GOLD!

I spent the next five months with Karl and Mike in their extremely comfortable self-contained flat, serving as a much-needed sanctuary and I was very grateful to have their company and support. It was also a time when I could get myself back on my feet again, financially, having left Hong Kong with much of the initial equity capital greatly diminished. I also took the opportunity to renew my close friendships with Michelle and Mike and family, as well as Andrew and Glen in London.

My immediate appointment was with the Royal Bournemouth Hospital and feeling a great deal of apprehension going to the Men's Health Clinic for the first time. My fears were, nevertheless, short-lived as I was treated with the utmost dignity and care, and with great sensitivity and kindness by the staff of the clinic, and it was yet another reminder of how fortunate we were to have such a magnificent NHS, free at the point of delivery. Following blood tests, the Clinic's Duty Doctor explained that as my cell count was relatively high, it would not be necessary for me to go on to anti-viral treatment at that stage. However, I would need to undergo regular check-ups every six months to monitor the situation. I remember thinking to myself at that time how incredibly fortunate I was. Had it been 25 years earlier, I could have suffered the same fate as Freddie Mercury and 20 million other young men and women and become just another very cruel and sad statistic. This being so poignantly and brilliantly portrayed many years later in the award-winning television series, "It's a sin".

Saga kept me busy over this period with new tours to South America and Cuba. But in spite of this, I was missing the 'buzz' of Hong Kong terribly and within a few months felt a very strong urge to return. When sharing this with friends and family, they expressed a degree of shock and dismay as to why I would want to return to a place connected with so much personal pain. But before I knew it, I had high-tailed it and was on a flight back.

I had already pre-booked a Service Apartment (the equivalent to a reasonably low-priced hotel) in the Central district for the first two months, and very soon was forming a small circle of friends. I was, however, very concerned that I might one day accidentally bump into Georges, but I never saw him again although subsequently heard he had settled permanently overseas with a new partner. One of the people who became a good friend was Dr Michael Lo, together with his lovely wife, Rita, a wine connoisseur and Japanese cookery expert.

Within the first month, I had also enrolled at a Fitness First gym which was vastly different from my Hawaiian experience of swaying palm trees and golden sands. Instead, a view of a large skyscraper building with a thousand circular holes that were apparently part of the architectural feature. It was often rumoured to be a place where a 'thousand arseholes' worked, although I never chose to find out.

Trina (Jenny Kellaway's daughter), who by now was in her late thirties and had kept in touch with me over the years, came to visit me for two weeks during that time, and I was only too pleased to play host and show her around what by now had become my adopted city and we had a great time together. By that time Trina had divorced her first husband, John, and a few years later would meet Paul Case, whom she would go on to marry.

Hong Kong quickly began to feel like home, and I embraced it fully. It's exhilarating, almost 24/7 atmosphere, a place where East meets West, its forest of cathedral-like skyscraper buildings, the sound of trundling street trams, the spectacular neon lighting of Victoria Harbour and breath-taking views from the tallest point in the city, 'The Peak'. The advertising strapline at the time: 'Live it! Love it!' seemed to perfectly sum up my feelings. Now fully convinced that I would stay permanently for the foreseeable future, with the help of a Chinese Hong Kong good friend Lung, I found a newly furnished one–bedroomed apartment to rent in a recently completed building block in an area called Sheung Wan, close to the central hub of the city.

Saga also continued to keep me fully occupied, mainly with China tours but also undertaking two of a newly launched adventure tour to Mongolia, renowned as the land of the mighty Mongol Empire and its conquering leader, Genghis

Khan. A beautiful, unspoilt country where clients and I slept under a 'Ger' or 'Yurt' – a typical Mongolian home; a wooden lattice structure, wrapped by a thin cover and insulated with layers of felt, and enjoying the exceptional hospitality and friendship of the mainly nomadic local tribes living in the Gobi Desert.

Given my disposition towards young Asian men in their late twenties/early thirties, Hong Kong was a veritable 'honeypot' for me (like some young testosterone-pumped kid let loose in Willy Wonka's Chocolate Factory!). I had formed a number of relationships by now with guys having a preference for more mature Caucasian men (known locally as 'Gweilos'). It was a period when my casual fun was bordering on a rather 'hedonistic' lifestyle and my libido working overtime, aided and abetted by 'Viagra'! These young men would invariably refer to mature Western men, like myself, as 'Daddy'.

Having undergone, several years earlier, three operations in the UK to deal with a persistent abscess problem on my rear end, I was shocked to suddenly find that the problem had returned, causing me excruciating pain. I had no option other than to get private treatment, including surgery, overnight hospital stay and post-operative treatment. It was not just a blow to me physically, but financially, with a final princely sum of £3,000 for medical services, wiping out all my savings at that time.

One day, unexpectedly, during my fifth year in Hong Kong, I received some exciting news from Trina who emailed me to say that she and husband Paul had found positions with Hong Kong companies and would be relocating to the city. Paul had secured a position as Vice-President of a large International Engineering Company and Trina as a Vice-President of Communications of a large Insurance Group. This was very welcome news for me. Paul and Trina subsequently moved into a large, rented house in the New Territories where over time I became a regular visitor.

Paul was a fairly tall, upright, handsome man, very masculine in appearance and in his early forties. He was a very proud and highly principled person, occasionally temperamental, but who was very considerate and caring and it was clear to me very early on how utterly devoted he was to Trina.

Trina and Paul had tried unsuccessfully for many years to have children, but eventually decided to adopt locally, although they were both in their late forties by the time their application had been accepted by the Hong Kong Welfare Department. Their first child was a girl, two years old, whom they called Martha. She was ethnically Hong Kong Chinese and who I would always call 'Princess'. Two years later, they adopted their second child, a boy of mixed-race origins, part Indonesian and part Pakistani, who was just 18 months old whom they named Joshua. I would call him 'Screamalot', simply because he did scream a lot at that time!

Trina and Paul were incredibly devoted parents, ensuring both of their children were given every opportunity to develop, and Paul in particular was determined to have them grow in an environment where traditional family values were upheld. Over the next few years, I would stay with Trina and Paul often for quite long spells, having the privilege of seeing both children mature and quickly acquiring the mantle

'Uncle Bill'. Every year, Trina and Paul would thoughtfully insist that I spend the Christmas holiday with them even if they were entertaining family members at the same time and thus in so many ways becoming my 'family' in Hong Kong.

During my latter years in the city, I began to fall into a familiar routine which, fed by OCD (Obsessive, Compulsive Disorder) mentality, I imagined must have driven Sally crazy, as well as my irritating fastidiousness. I chose to eat out most days and would always take lunch in an auspiciously named restaurant, 'The Queen's', which had a gay owner, Joseph. It was here that I was adopted and spoiled by the three wonderfully attentive female staff, Cecille, Theresa and Arnia, where a reserved table was kept for me every day. Arnia, who would normally serve me was always rather cheeky and would greet me each day with the same opening line: "Uncle Bill, what's it going to be today? Beer for a queer or wine for a wanker?". And who said that the Chinese didn't have a sense of humour!

I was also delighted that my lovely niece, Sharon, whom I had reconnected with after an absence of several years on one of my visits back to the UK, came to Hong Kong for a brief long weekend visit and we were able to meet up at her hotel for dinner.

Other friends who visited me during this time were Jilly, Andrew and Glen, Karl and Mike, and Suzi and John.

One of my really close local gay friends was an American man, Dave. He lived with his long-term partner, Stephen, a Hong Kong Chinese guy who was a teacher by profession, whereas Dave worked for a fibre optics American Company and was their Chinese representative. Dave was a man in his late thirties, bald headed and very large, physically, but having a generous nature and heart to match, whom I had met when I first took an apartment in Sheung Wan. Although he was a self-confessed, avowed 'Trump' supporter, I never allowed that to interfere with our friendship. We often met for breakfast or lunch, invariably over a good 'Victor Meldrew' moan, particularly about obscenely paid Hedge Fund Managers and footballers, but avoiding where we could the mention of the name 'Trump'. Many friends who would often be subjected to one of my long-winded 'rants', frequently interrupted me with: "Wouldn't it be so wonderful, Bill, if you ruled the world". This being my cue to shut up!

Dave once confessed to me that when on a trip to the movies with Stephen to watch 'Love, actually', featuring the multi-talented actor, Bill Nighy, playing the role of an ageing 'rocker', as he appeared for the first time on the screen, they each turned to each other and said: "It's Uncle Bill!". It seemed I had moved on from Peter O'Toole.

Another rather self-pitying "why me?" moment (and yet a further price to be paid for my earlier heavy smoking habit), was when I had to have most of my front upper teeth removed and fitted with dentures, something I absolutely hated. Whenever I was touring, I sounded like a mixture of 'Donald Duck' or a whistling kettle! Fortuitously, Paul knew locally, a leading periodontics dental surgeon, Dr Sandeep, a truly kind and sensitive man, originally from India. Within months he had replaced my dentures with permanent implants at a much-discounted cost, but still wiping out all my savings and much of my earnings for the following year.

But at least I had my smile back and my vanity restored.

In the late summer of 2017, I had an email from Makala, informing me that she had found another position within the Company and would be leaving her current post. By that time, Makala had been my Line Manager for 16 years and had always allocated me a good selection of tours every year. A male replacement came in shortly afterwards, but I had already made the decision to hang up the clipboard for the last time the following year, by that time aged 75 and with already enough miles on the clock. I would, however, remain eternally grateful to Saga, but most especially to Anna Collins (who by that time, had also left the Company) as many years earlier, she had opened a completely new and exciting door for me leading to countless happy and fulfilling memories.

After several abortive efforts to re-settle back in England, only to be lured back to Hong Kong again, I knew that having finally given up my self-employed work with Saga and with just a pension to live on, I quickly came to the conclusion that I could no longer continue to afford to stay in a city that had become my adopted home for the past 17 years. To contribute to this decision was that in early 2018, following one of my six-monthly check-ups at the health clinic in Bournemouth, I was strongly advised to return to the UK and immediately go onto a course of anti-viral medication as my cell count had dropped quite dramatically.

With my imminent move to England, Trina and Paul made an offer that would prove to be mutually beneficial and with perfect timing. Trina's parents had both sadly died over the previous three years and left their large furnished family home in Parkstone, Poole, to Trina and they wanted me to 'house sit' for them and serve as a quasi-project manager whilst major improvement work was undertaken. This was to commence from late March the following year and for a period of approximately 18 months, before they planned to re-settle back in the house, hoping it would be virtually refurbished by that time.

This generous offer coincided with increasing concerns I had about Hong Kong. It was no longer the 'Live it! Love it!' City I had fallen for when I first settled some 17 years earlier. The increasing and very transparent disparity between the 'haves' and 'have nots' had become so much part of everyday life and lent truth to the saying: "All that glitters is not necessarily gold". I had become very disillusioned with the social injustices and general 'elitism', with an increasingly draconian Government committed only to ensuring that the 'status quo' was maintained, enabling rich tycoons and big corporations to benefit at the expense of ordinary citizens. There were thousands of young people struggling to save enough for a mortgage whilst forced to live in highly expensive sub-divided apartments. Moreover, thousands more who had no option but to live in what were termed 'cages'. Yet, paradoxically, Hong Kong was one of the world's richest cities. But now, demonstrably, developing into a Dystopian society with increasing surveillance and violation of human rights.

These injustices had also promoted a rather selfish and self-centred attitude amongst some wealthier Hong Kong people, with the retention of full-time domestic helpers, principally from the Philippines (the modern-day equivalent to indentured slavery) with abysmally poor pay and often shocking accommodation and working conditions. These attitudes were also exacerbated by mainstream education with its almost exclusive emphasis on academic achievement, rather than individual life and social skills elements. Money had also become virtually a form of 'deity', along with the obsessive addiction to the use of iPhones.

So, towards the end of March 2019, I left Hong Kong, possibly for the last time, with very mixed emotions as I made my way to Chek Lap Kok Airport (designed by the famous architect Norman Foster) to spend what remaining years I had left, back home in my own country of birth, England.

Niece Sharon and me in Hong Kong

LOCKDOWNS AND SOCIAL DISTANCING

As I had envisaged, it took me some time to adjust to my new surroundings in Parkstone. Situated between the towns of Poole and Bournemouth, the 100-metre driveway led down to the house, designed and built 50 years earlier by Trina's talented father, Stan, a very well respected and distinguished local architect. It enjoyed a prominent position perched on a hillside and surrounded by a woodland of tall deciduous trees within a very expansive, but overgrown garden, complete with dried up pond. As I was also soon to discover, a sanctuary for squirrels, two fox families and a variety of different bird species and the occasional uninvited interloper!

The major internal works started almost immediately, and it was at times challenging living in an environment cheek by jowl with builders every weekday, invariably involving very early starts, but I was nevertheless exceedingly grateful to Trina and Paul for giving me the opportunity of re-settling back in the UK, virtually rent-free. There were several times early on, however, when I reminisced over my former carefree halcyon days back in Hong Kong.

It was, nevertheless, a great consolation to be re-united with friends and family (particularly feeling at one point I may have burnt my bridges), especially friends Michelle and Mike and their by now quite grown up children. Within the first couple of months, I also headed up to the lovely 'village like' Crouch End in North London to pay a visit to Andrew and Glen. I was pleasantly surprised to find that Andrew had become quite an accomplished portrait artist and had secured several commissions. Glen, meanwhile, was still the lead violinist with the English National Opera Orchestra. I was also meeting Denise for lunch every week with whom I had formed a close friendship, together with husband Wim. And I also managed a trip over to Chelmsford to see Darryl and Jackie and to meet for the first time their handsome, very sporty, teenage son, Harrison. I always felt true friendships were those that, despite the passage of time, picked up from where they left off, and that was certainly true of my experiences.

My very caring niece, Sharon, and her husband, Nigel and their super family, had become particularly close to me and I spent many extended weekends with them at their beautiful home in Woking. But somehow, I had still not summed up sufficient confidence to 'take to the boards' again and re-join Bournemouth Little Theatre Club.

Adapting to a quite dramatic change in climate also took time, but more significantly, I felt a number of seismic changes, some cultural, had evolved since leaving Bournemouth nearly two decades earlier. I was quite shocked by the level of obesity, especially amongst younger people, which had reached almost epidemic proportions and having also re-joined a gym, the proneness towards tattoos and body piercings, together with the adoption of beards and moustaches. Most alarming was that I found Bournemouth (a very popular seaside resort), especially the town centre, distinctly dirty and littered, even in streets renowned for upmarket retail businesses, with many rough sleepers. Generally, there seemed to be an increasing disregard for civic pride.

Television programmes had also, in my view, pandered to the lowest common denominator, especially in the field of comedy, although I was pleased to see that other favourites like 'Antiques Road Show' and 'Strictly Come Dancing' had survived and I welcomed new programmes like 'The Repair Shop' and 'Gogglebox'. But I despaired that the relatively new cult of 'celebrity' status (often talentless individuals) had flourished, serving as a platform for preposterous, self-indulgent and quite depressing 'reality' television programmes.

What concerned me more was what I felt to be a general lack of tolerance and a growing climate of anti-social behaviour, and not just confined to young people who were, more often than not, demonised by society. There seemed to be an expanding and widespread obsession with a rather selfish 'Me, Me, I, I' attitude and a greater obsession with 'rights' rather than 'responsibilities'. Moreover, youth crime had increased exponentially over the past 20 years, correspondingly at a time when savage Government cuts in youth service provision had been implemented, leading to the disappearance of many neighbourhood youth centres, thus driving many young people back onto the streets and into potentially recalcitrant behaviour. Much of the police body-cam programmes I was witnessing on television only served to reinforce these fears. It was further alarming to find that youth suicides, especially amongst young men, were higher than since records first began.

Adapting to a 'Western' culture again after so many years' absence was also a time of adjustment for me. In particular, I was really quite surprised to find that many English young people were being generalised and depicted as part of a 'snowflake' generation – lacking determination and less resilient. Yet, my limited experience led me to believe that if this meant they were exercising greater awareness and sensitivity, this could, in my view, only be seen as a positive development.

I had also hoped that after nearly a twenty-year absence, more significant advances would have been made in the area of discrimination and prejudice. Sadly, this did not always appear to be the case. I had a very bad experience shortly after re-settling in the UK when travelling back by bus one night, quite late, after attending a concert. Four lads, around 18 or 19 years of age, boarded the bus and were clearly the worst for drink and immediately started swinging on the overhead grab handles. Despite the driver stopping the bus twice and issuing severe warnings, their bad behaviour then descended into a torrent of homophobic, misogynistic, Islamophobic and racists rants. I eventually challenged the lads, only to be subjected to a great deal of personal abuse. Subsequently, I heard how common this kind of thing was and yet could not understand why in the 21st century we were not adopting 'zero tolerance' attitudes to such offensive and unacceptable behaviour. I felt that sport, in particular, needed to stop paying 'lip service' and rather than simply suspend (in many cases highly paid individuals) but ban for life any offenders. If it took draconian measures to bring about a radical mind-set change and to confront, and eventually, eliminate this malignant behaviour, so be it, as far as I was concerned.

I was also surprised to find that the obsession with the iPhone had been embraced, similarly to Hong Kong, and finding myself constantly irritated by people on the bus who indulged in loud conversations on their mobile phone, which fellow passengers couldn't help but overhear. It reminded me of the humorous joke told by the much-loved and sadly departed comedian, Victoria Wood. This was about a couple in a fully occupied train compartment conspicuously love-making, with other fellow passengers choosing to ignore this. Having finished, the couple then proceeded to light up a cigarette, when one of the passengers looked up from his newspaper and said, "Excuse me, do you mind, this is a non-smoking compartment!".

It was also a shock for me to find that the expression I had used over the past 25 years, 'darling', and one which I had always considered purely as a term of endearment, irrespective as to whether it was directed at a male or female, could be challenged as 'sexist' by a new breed of what were termed 'woke warriors'!

As a person who had grown up with Clark Gable and Audrey Hepburn as role models, I had always endeavoured to sartorially maintain high standards, and yet was now finding that a 'dress-down' code had been widely adopted. Of course, I recognised, given my age, that this was a generational problem, but it made the transition into my final 'twilight zone' years unsettling.

There were, however, some advantageous benefits to my maturing years. I qualified for a free bus pass, saving me at least £100 a month. Furthermore, a long-awaited hernia operation, diagnosed eight years earlier, was carried out in mid-2020 and was a further example of how fortunate we were to have the NHS. But with my seventy-eighth year on the horizon, my health had gradually and incrementally deteriorated, despite my regular gym fitness regime. My respiratory problems had now been fully diagnosed as C.O.P.D. (Chronic Obstructive Pulmonary Disease), so, inevitably, tackling steps and steep inclines were becoming increasingly difficult. A further reminder that my earlier smoking habit had returned to bite me in the bum (or something like that!). But at least I was delighted to be re-united with my favourite classical radio station, Classic FM.

Nevertheless, my 'Peter Pan' life-long obsession was now having a much overdue reality check. Every month, the appearance of yet more lumps and bumps, aches and pains, to say nothing of facial wrinkles, were now prominent features of daily life and also over a period when I had to undergo an eye laser operation for cataracts. All this, together with increasing 'senior moment' memory lapses, yet at the same time faced with the dichotomy of constantly being reminded that no matter how young the brain still thought it was, the body had distinctly different ideas!

Boris Johnson was somebody I could never take seriously, even more so when assuming the Premiership in the summer of 2019. Hardly a role model for the UK hairdressing industry and as one newspaper diarist wryly once observed, 'Like Ken Dodd having a bad hair day!' Yet, neither he, nor the rest of the world's population, could have predicted that the following year, 2020, would become an unprecedented and critical life-changing moment for humanity.

It was the discovery of a deadly disease, Coronavirus (Covid-19), allegedly emanating from a wet market in Wuhan, China, a city I had visited many times, being the starting point for Saga's China tours up the Yangtze River. Over the next two years life changed dramatically for everyone, creating a surreal environment and whilst not discriminatory, my age-group were especially vulnerable to this fatal disease. What began as an epidemic rapidly became a pandemic and by mid-2021, over 2.5 million people worldwide had become victims, with 140,000 deaths and rising in the UK alone.

There were three national lockdowns over the next 18 months and terms like social distancing, tiers, shielding, Stay at Home, Protect the NHS, Save Lives, PPE, furloughing, took on an ominous everyday language of its own, and national scientists and health officials would become familiar household names. It was especially hard for all young people, particularly those whose schooling and university study was severely disrupted.

Close by towns like Bournemouth and Poole became almost overnight eerily ghost-like during protracted lockdowns, with all but essential retail outlets closed, and hospitality venues like pubs and hotels taking the brunt of the emergency measures introduced by the Government.

Like everyone else, there were times when I felt desperately lonely, my hair almost at shoulder length, my waist-line expanding and feeling somehow that the future had been cancelled. A time, however, when I was very thankful for technology, as my niece Sharon, friends Michelle, Junior, Andrew and Glen and many others kept up my spirits, regularly sharing Facetime video calls as well as telephone conversations, and thus saving my sanity.

On one occasion when 'normality' had resumed, albeit temporarily, I was stopped one day in Bournemouth Town Square by a 'Big Issue' seller for an autograph, convinced I was the actor Larry Lamb of 'EastEnders' fame. It seemed I had moved on from Peter and Bill with my new guise keeping pace with my many adopted nicknames.

It was also a realisation that everyday behaviour we all took for granted – hugging, kissing, a simple human touch – were suppressed, admittedly temporarily, and the wearing of masks and exercising social distancing almost everywhere, mandatory. For a 'touchy feely' person like myself, it was especially frustrating. Furthermore, it was also a wake-up call, if ever it were needed, of the dedication of front-line workers, particularly those in the NHS, many of whom themselves fell victim to the deadly disease.

There were, however, also countless acts of kindness and altruism. Over Christmas 2020, due to a last-minute lockdown, I found myself inadvertently alone on Christmas Day, unprepared, and yet in spite of her own very busy schedule and family needs, Michelle still took time out to deliver to me a full Christmas lunch. Also, often in times of despair and despondency, national heroes emerged and none more so than the inspiring Captain Tom Moore. A centenarian, who with the aid of his Zimmer, walked 100 lengths of his garden, unleashing worldwide support and raising nearly £33 million for the NHS. Captain Tom went on to be knighted by the Queen, yet tragically died in February 2021 from coronavirus.

But he left behind a remarkable legacy and his indomitable spirit would live on.

After the second lockdown, Trina and Paul contacted me to say that they would be returning permanently to the UK in September 2020, although they fully understood that there was still a great deal of outstanding building work to be completed, much of which had been interrupted by the previous lockdowns. The house, of course, holding strong emotional ties for Trina.

I immediately set about looking for a furnished apartment and was very fortunate to quickly fall on my feet, acquiring a very elegant and sophisticated small apartment very close to Bournemouth town centre that ticked all my boxes. It was located in a building block that had undergone major refurbishment called 'Queens House', which some of my friends felt was highly appropriate. Within this delightful furnished apartment was a constant reminder of my China tours – a life size statue of a terracotta warrior, complete with spear, that my very kind Spanish flat owner had shipped back from a visit to Xian he had made several years earlier. At long last I could claim to having a companion, 'Terry' – although not a great conversationalist but at least a 'live in' partner!

Having led a somewhat 'nomadic' lifestyle, my elder sister, Barbara, commented that she had literally filled her address book with all my location changes over the years and hoped I would settle down at long last. Whether or not I would remain in my new apartment was difficult to predict, but one thing was very certain, England would, without doubt, remain my permanent right of abode.

After a few months in my new apartment, I had also reunited with a gay friend from over 20 years earlier, Lawrence. He had spent many years in Los Angeles before returning to England to set up home with a partner in London for ten years. Regrettably, their relationship broke down and he had settled back in Bournemouth eight years later.

By the middle of 2020, thanks to the dedication, ingenuity and brilliance of scientists worldwide, a radiant bright light began to shine at the end of what had become a very dark tunnel. At long last a pathway out of the crisis when once again 'hope sprung eternal' and several vaccines had been approved. By the beginning of 2021, a highly successful inoculation programme had been implemented with me having both jabs by April of that year. However, some restrictions remained in place but there was every expectation that by the summer, life would begin to take on some sense of normality again for everyone.

This was also a moment of reflection for me, as a gay person. Somehow I could not entirely reconcile myself to the unmistakable fact that it had taken science just over a year to produce a vaccine to stop the spread of Covid-19, with a death toll of over two million worldwide, yet it had been 30 years since the first appearance of HIV/Aids and despite the introduction of life-saving therapeutic treatment, such as anti-viral medication, over 20 million, mostly young and third world people, had been lost to this universal pandemic, but still no vaccines had yet been developed to prevent the spread of this pernicious disease.

For someone who had spent a major part of his life involved with youth work, it was also a very sad moment for me when news of the Duke of Edinburgh's death was announced in April 2021. As well as being the longest serving consort to the Queen, he had established the highly successful Duke of Edinburgh (D of E) Award Scheme which had benefited hundreds of thousands of young people across the globe and would go on to be his remarkable lasting legacy, as well as his spirited reputation.

In common with many others, I had genuine concerns for the future of humanity and our fragile planet, especially the ever-present conundrum of having to balance wealth creation with conservation, yet took inspiration from the likes of Sir David Attenborough and the young Greta Thunberg, who had not only raised awareness but campaigned tirelessly about the potential dangers of world pollution and global warming. I was also specifically concerned for young people, now living with the full implications of what increasing numbers felt to be the growing corrosive cesspits of social media – the promotion of hate speech, anonymous on-line trolling, self-harm platforms, cyberbullying – and thus the very urgent need for overdue regulation to prevent yet more vulnerable people falling victim.

After more than 55 years of extensive worldwide travel and clocking up neatly three-quarters of a million air miles, I had also come to the firm conclusion that despite different cultures, customs and languages, there was much more that united rather than divided us as a humanity. But alarmingly, irrespective of whether developed or developing nation, the gulf between the rich and poor had, from my observations, widened dramatically.

As I entered the remaining twilight zone years and virtually completing my own 'full circle of life', I was able to pause and look back on seven decades of living; contemplating its somewhat 'rollercoaster' nature and share of 'ups and downs', moments of triumph and disappointment, especially dark periods blighted by depression, anxiety, low self-esteem and the loss of my personal 'mojo', yet at the same time, hoping I had retained a good sense of humour throughout it all. The numerous opportunities presented to me, prompted by my dad's home-spun philosophy: "If you don't bloody well ask…!" The many times when doors suddenly closed, yet others opened, although not always perfectly synchronised. Despite increasing health problems, this did not signal a willingness on my part to 'exit stage left' with yet a couple more ticks remaining on my personal 'bucket list'.

Throughout my life, I had always kept faith with a somewhat egalitarian outlook and hoped that my internal moral compass had always enabled me to hold on to certain core values and principles with the overriding mantra, "Treat people in the same way you wished to be treated yourself". Although very acutely aware that I had fallen far short of that aspiration many times.

Whilst fortune, in purely monetary terms, had somehow always eluded me (primarily self-inflicted), I was able to genuinely claim a true 'richness' in the many close and intimate friendships I had established over my lifetime.

Overall, however, with almost one foot already in the grave, I still retained an optimistic, half-full, rather than half-empty outlook. But, more importantly, shared Captain Sir Tom Moore's watchword: "Tomorrow will be a good day".

"Princess" and me

www.ingramcontent.com/pod-product-compliance
Lightning Source LLC
Chambersburg PA
CBHW051648040426
42446CB00009B/1025